Psychological Modeling

Conflicting Theories

Edited by

Albert Bandura

ALDINETRANSACTION
A Division of Transaction Publishers
New Brunswick (U.S.A.) and London (U.K.)

Second printing 2007
Copyright © 1971 by Transaction Publishers, New Brunswick, New Jersey.

This book is printed on acid-free paper that meets the American National Standard for Permanence of Paper for Printed Library Materials.

Library of Congress Catalog Number: 2006045610
ISBN: 978-0-202-30848-7
Printed in the United States of America

Library of Congress Cataloging-in-Publication Data

Psychological modeling : conflicting theories / edited by Albert Bandura.
    p. cm.
  Includes bibliographical references and index.
  ISBN 0-202-30848-0 (pbk. : alk. paper)
  1. Learning, Psychology of. I. Bandura, Albert, 1925-

LB1051.B244 2006
370.15'23—dc22   2006045610

Psychological Modeling

Contents

PSYCHOLOGICAL MODELING

Analysis of Modeling Processes

ALBERT BANDURA

Among the numerous topics that have attracted the interest of psychologists over the years, the phenomenon of learning has occupied a central position. Most of the research in this area examines the process of learning as a consequence of direct experience: This volume is principally concerned with learning by example.

It is evident from informal observation that human behavior is transmitted, whether deliberately or inadvertently, largely through exposure to social models. Indeed, as Reichard (1938) noted some years ago, in many languages "the word for 'teach' is the same as the word for 'show'." It is difficult to imagine a culture in which language, mores, vocational activities, familial cus-

The preparation of this paper and research by the author which is reported here was facilitated by grants M–5162 and 1F03MH42658 from the National Institute of Mental Health, United States Public Health Service. The author also gratefully acknowledges the generous assistance of the staff of the Center for Advanced Study in the Behavioral Sciences.

1

toms, and educational, religious, and political practices are gradually shaped in each new member by direct consequences of their trial-and-error performances without benefit of models who display the cultural patterns in their behavior.

Although much social learning is fostered through observation of real-life models, advances in communication have increased reliance upon symbolic models. In many instances people pattern their behavior after models presented in verbal or pictorial form. Without the guidance of handbooks that describe in detail how to behave in particular situations, members of technologically advanced societies would spend much of their time groping for effective ways of handling situations that arise repeatedly. Pictorially presented models, provided in television and other filmed displays, also serve as influential sources of social behavior.

Considering the prevailing influence of example in the development and regulation of human behavior, it is surprising that traditional accounts of learning contain little or no mention of modeling processes. If the peripatetic Martian were to scrutinize earth man's authoritative texts on learning he would be left with the belief that there are two basic modes of learning: People are either conditioned through reward and punishment to adopt the desired patterns, or emotional responsiveness is established by close association of neutral and evocative stimuli. If these methods alone were applied on the distant planet, the life span of Martians would not only be drastically shortened, but their brief period of survival would be expended in prolonged and laborious efforts to master simple skills.

The marked discrepancy between textbook and social reality is largely attributable to the fact that certain critical conditions present in natural situations are rarely, if ever, reproduced in laboratory studies of learning. In laboratory investigations experimenters arrange comparatively benign environments in which errors do not create fatal consequences for the organism. By contrast, natural environments are loaded with potentially lethal consequences for those unfortunate enough to perform hazardous errors. For this reason it would be exceedingly injudicious to rely on differential reinforcement of trial-and-error performances in teaching children to swim, adolescents to drive automobiles, medical students to conduct surgical operations, or adults to develop complex occupational and social competencies. Had experimental situations been made more realistic so that animals toiling in Skinner boxes and various mazes were drowned, electrocuted, dismembered, or extensively bruised for the errors that invariably occur during early phases of unguided learning, the limitations of instrumental conditioning would have been forcefully revealed.

There are several reasons why modeling influences are heavily favored in promoting everyday learning. Under circumstances in which mistakes are costly or dangerous, skillful performances can be established without needless errors by providing competent models who demonstrate the required activities. Some complex behaviors can be produced solely through the influence of models. If children had no opportunity to hear speech it would be virtually impossible to teach them the linguistic skills that constitute a language. It is doubtful whether one could ever shape individual words by selective reinforcement of random vocalizations, let alone grammatical utterances. Where desired forms of behavior can be conveyed only by social cues, modeling is an indispensable aspect of learning. Even in instances where it is possible to establish new response patterns through other means, the process of acquisition can be considerably shortened by providing appropriate models (Bandura & McDonald, 1963; John, Chesler, Bartlett, & Victor, 1968; Luchins & Luchins, 1966).

Differentiation of Modeling Phenomena

Modeling phenomena have been differentiated, and much time has been spent in conflict over the criteria used in these arbitrary classifications. Among the diverse terms applied to matching behavior are "imitation," "modeling," "observational learning,"

"identification," "internalization," "introjection," "incorpora-
tion," "copying," "social facilitation," "contagion," and "role-
taking."

In theoretical discussions imitation is most frequently differentiated from identification on the basis of the content of the
changes resulting from exposure to modeling influences. Imitation is generally defined as the reproduction of discrete responses, but there is little agreement concerning the use of the
term identification. Different writers have ascribed to identification the adoption of either diverse patterns of behavior (Kohlberg, 1963; Parsons, 1955; Stoke, 1950), symbolic representation of the model (Emmerich, 1959), similar meaning systems
(Lazowick, 1955), or motives, values, ideals, and conscience
(Gewirtz & Stingle, 1968).

Distinctions are sometimes made in terms of the conditions assumed to produce and maintain matching behavior, as illustrated
by Parsons's (1951) view that "a generalized cathectic attach-
ment" is required for identification, but is unnecessary in imitation. Kohlberg (1963) differs in reserving the term identification
for matching behavior that is presumed to be maintained by intrinsic satisfactions derived from perceived similarity, and apply-
ing the label imitation to instrumental matching responses supported by extrinsic rewards. Others define imitation as matching
behavior occurring in the presence of the model, and identification as performance of the model's behavior in his absence
(Kohlberg, 1963; Mowrer, 1950). Not only is there little con-
sensus with respect to differentiating criteria, but some theorists
assume that imitation produces identification, while others contend with equally strong conviction that identification results in
imitation.

Unless it can be shown that modeling of different forms of behavior is governed by separate determinants, distinctions proposed in terms of the content of what is emulated not only are
gratuitous, but may cause needless confusion. Limited progress
would be made in understanding learning processes if fundamentally different mechanisms were invoked, without empirical justi-

fication, to account for the acquisition of one social response versus ten social responses that are arbitrarily designated as elements of a role. Results of numerous studies reviewed in detail elsewhere (Bandura, 1969a) reveal that the same determinants influence acquisition of isolated matching responses and of entire behavioral repertoires in identical ways. Moreover, retention and delayed reproduction of even discrete matching responses require symbolic representation of previously modeled events, especially in early stages of learning. There is also little reason to suppose on empirical or on theoretical grounds that the principles and processes involved in the acquisition of modeled behaviors later performed in the presence of models are different from those performed in their absence.

Several experiments (Bandura, Blanchard & Ritter, 1969; Blanchard, 1970; Perloff, 1970) have demonstrated that exposure to the same modeling influence simultaneously produces in observers analogous changes in specific behavior, emotional responsiveness, valuation of objects involved in the modeled activities, and in self-evaluation. It may be questioned whether any conceptual benefits accrue from arbitrarily designating some of these changes as identification and others as imitation. Indeed, if the diverse criteria enumerated above were seriously applied either singly or in various combinations in categorizing modeling outcomes, most instances of matching behavior that have been traditionally labeled imitation would also qualify as identification, and much of the behavior cited as identificatory learning would be reclassified as imitation.

In social learning theory (Bandura, 1969a) the phenomena ordinarily subsumed under the labels imitation and identification are designated as *modeling*. The latter term was adopted because modeling influences have much broader psychological effects than the simple response mimicry implied by the term imitation, and the distinguishing properties of identification are too diffuse, arbitrary, and empirically questionable either to clarify issues or to aid scientific inquiry. Research conducted within this framework has shown that modeling influences can produce three separable types of effects depending on the different processes involved. First, observers can acquire new patterns of behavior by watching the performances of others. This *observational learning effect* is demonstrated most clearly when models exhibit novel responses which observers have not yet learned to make and which they later reproduce in substantially identical form.

A second major function of modeling influences is to strengthen or to weaken inhibition of previously learned responses. The effects that modeled activities have on behavioral restraints are largely determined by observation of rewarding and punishing consequences accompanying the actions. *Inhibitory effects* are indicated when observers show either decrements in the modeled class of behavior or a general reduction of responsiveness as a result of seeing the model's behavior produce punishing consequences. Observed punishment has been shown to reduce exploratory behavior (Crooks, 1967), aggression (Bandura, 1965b; Wheeler, 1966), and transgressive behavior (Walters & Parke, 1964; Walters, Parke & Cane, 1965). Comparable reductions in performance are obtained in observers when models respond self-punitively to their own behavior (Bandura, 1971a; Benton, 1967).

Disinhibitory effects are evident when observers increase performance of formerly inhibited behavior after observing models engage in threatening or prohibited activities without adverse consequences. This type of change is most strikingly illustrated in the treatment of phobic conditions through modeling procedures (Bandura, 1971b). People who strongly inhibit even attenuated approach responses toward objects they fear are able to interact closely with them after observing bold performers engaging in threatening activities without experiencing any untoward consequences.

The behavior of others can also serve as cues in facilitating performance of existing responses in the same general class. People applaud when others clap; they look up when they see others gazing skyward; they adopt fads that others display; and in countless other situations their behavior is prompted and channeled by the actions of others. *Response facilitation effects* are distinguished from observational learning and disinhibition because no new responses are acquired, and disinhibitory processes are not involved because the behavior in question is socially sanctioned and hence is unemcumbered by restraints.

EXPLANATORY THEORIES

Some of the major controversies in the explanation of modeling phenomena can best be illustrated by tracing the evolution of theories of imitation. Disputes between theoretical positions often arise from failure to distinguish the diverse effects that modeling influences can have. Since different conditions are required to produce observational learning, modification of behavioral restraints, and social facilitation, a theory proposed to explain learning by observation will necessarily differ from one that is principally concerned with social facilitation. A number of other important issues that are raised by current theorizing and research will be discussed later.

Instinctual Interpretations

The earliest explanations of imitation (Morgan, 1896; Tarde, 1903; and McDougall, 1908) regarded modeling as instinctual: People reproduce the behavior of others because they have an innate propensity to do so. As the practice of attributing human behavior to instinctual forces gained widespread acceptance, psychologists became increasingly critical of the explanatory value of the instinct concept. Subsequent theories assumed that imitativeness is acquired through some type of learning mechanism, though they differed as to what is learned and the factors considered essential for imitation to occur.

Associative Theories

After the instinct doctrine fell into disrepute, a number of psychologists, notably Humphrey (1921), Allport (1924), Holt

(1931), and Guthrie (1952), portrayed modeling in terms of associative principles. As Guthrie succinctly stated, "If we have performed an act, the stimuli associated with that act tend to become cues for its performance (p. 287)." Associative learning was believed to be achieved most rapidly through initial reverse imitation. According to Holt's conceptualization, when an adult copies the response of a child, the latter tends to repeat the reiterated behavior. As this circular associative sequence continues, the adult's behavior becomes an increasingly effective stimulus for the child's responses. If during this spontaneous mutual imitation the adult performs a response that is novel for the child, he will copy it. Piaget (1952) likewise cited imitations at early stages of development in which the child's spontaneous behaviors serve initially as stimuli for matching responses by the model in alternating imitative sequences. Allport believed that imitativeness develops through classical conditioning of verbalizations, motor responses, or emotions to similar classes of social stimuli with which they have been contiguously associated.

The associative theories explained how previously learned behavior might be elicited by the actions of others. But the principle of association does not adequately account for the fact that behavior is controlled by some social stimuli, but not by others that have been associated with equal frequency. A more serious limitation is the failure of these formulations to explain how novel responses are learned to begin with. Observational learning in humans and animals does not ordinarily commence by having a model reproduce irrelevant responses of the learner. In using modeling procedures to teach a myna bird to talk, for example, the trainer does not engage initially in circular crowing behavior; he begins by uttering words he wishes to teach that clearly do not exist in integrated form in the bird's vocal repertoire.

Reinforcement Theories

With the advent of reinforcement principles, the emphasis in learning theory shifted from classical conditioning to instrumental conditioning based on reinforcing consequences. Theories of modeling similarly assumed that observational learning occurred through reinforcement of imitative behavior. Learning was still conceptualized in terms of the formation of associations between social stimuli and matching responses, but reinforcement was added as the selective factor determining which of the many responses displayed by others will be imitated.

The foremost proponents of behaviorism, Watson (1908) and Thorndike (1898), dismissed the existence of observational learning on the basis of disappointing results from a few animals tested under conditions in which observation of the demonstrator's performance was not adequately controlled. Since the theories in vogue at the time assumed that learning required performance of responses, the notion of learning by observation alone was perhaps too divergent to be given serious consideration.

There was no research to speak of on modeling processes until the publication of the classic *Social Learning and Imitation* by Miller and Dollard in 1941. They advanced the view that in order for imitative learning to occur, observers must be motivated to act, modeling cues for the requisite behavior must be provided, observers must perform matching responses, and they must be positively reinforced. It was further assumed that if imitative behavior is repeatedly rewarded, imitation itself becomes a secondary drive presumably reduced by acting like the model.

The experiments conducted by Miller and Dollard demonstrated that when subjects are consistently rewarded for imitating the choice responses of a model in two-choice discrimination problems, they show a marked increase in imitativeness, but cease imitating the model if they are never rewarded for making the same choices. Moreover, subjects generalize copying responses to new models and to different motivational states. No attempt was made, however, to test whether imitation functions as a drive, which presumably should be altered in strength by deprivation or satiation of matching behavior.

These experiments have been widely accepted as demonstrations of imitative learning although they actually represent only a special form of discrimination place-learning in which social rather than environmental cues serve as stimuli for choice responses that already exist in the subject's behavioral repertoire. Indeed, had a light or some other distinctive cue been used to signify the outcomes of choices, the behavior of models would have been irrelevant, perhaps even a hindrance, to efficient performance. By contrast, most forms of imitation involve *response* rather than *place-learning,* in which observers organize behavioral elements into new compound responses solely by observing modeled performances. Since Miller and Dollard's theory requires a person to perform imitative responses before he can learn them, it accounts more adequately for the expression of previously established matching responses than for their acquisition. It is perhaps for this reason that the publication of *Social Learning and Imitation,* which contained many provocative ideas, stimulated little new research, and modeling processes continued to be treated in a cursory fashion or ignored entirely in accounts of learning.

The operant conditioning analysis of modeling phenomena (Baer & Sherman, 1964; Skinner, 1953), which also specifies reinforcement as a necessary condition, relies entirely upon the standard three-component paradigm $S^d \rightarrow R \rightarrow R^r$, where S^d denotes the modeled stimulus, R represents an overt matching response, and S^r designates the reinforcing stimulus. Except for deletion of the motivational requirement, the Skinnerian interpretation contains the same necessary conditions for imitation (that is, cue, response, reinforcement) originally proposed by Miller and Dollard. Observational learning is presumed to be achieved through a process of differential reinforcement. When imitative behavior has been positively reinforced and divergent responses either not rewarded or punished, the behavior of others comes to function as discriminative stimuli for matching responses.

It is difficult to see how this scheme applies to the observational learning that takes place without overt performance of the model's responses during the acquisition phase, without reinforcers administered to the model or to the observer, and in which the first appearance of the acquired response may be delayed for days, weeks, or even months. In the latter case, which represents one of the most prevalent forms of social learning, two of the events ($R \rightarrow S^r$) in the three-term paradigm are absent during acquisition, and the third element (S^d, or modeling stimulus) is typically absent from the situation in which the observationally learned response is performed. Like the Miller and Dollard theory, the Skinnerian interpretation explains how performance of established matching responses is facilitated by social stimuli and reinforcing consequences. It does not adequately explain how a new matching response is acquired observationally in the first place. This occurs through symbolic processes during the period of exposure to modeling stimuli, prior to overt responding or the appearance of any reinforcing events.

In a recent operant conditioning analysis of generalized imitation, Gewirtz and Stingle (1968) conceptualized observational learning as analogous to the matching-to-sample paradigm used to study discrimination learning. In this procedure a subject chooses from among a number of comparison stimuli one that shares a common property with the sample stimulus. Although modeling and matching-to-sample performances both involve a matching process, they can hardly be equated. A person can achieve errorless choices in matching comparison Italian and Wagnerian operatic arias with a sample Wagnerian recital, but remain totally unable to perform the vocal behavior contained in the sample. Accurate stimulus discrimination is merely a precondition for observational response learning.

In reducing observational learning to operant conditioning, Gewirtz usually cites examples in which models simply facilitate previously learned responses. However, the purpose of a theory of observational learning is not to account for social facilitation of established responses, but to explain how observers can acquire a novel response that they have never made before as a result of observing a model. Gewirtz argues that since the entire past learning history of an observer is not known, one cannot prove the negative: that a given response had not been learned prior to the modeling experience. That people can learn by observation can be readily demonstrated without controlling or cataloguing the entire life history of the observer. One need only model an original response, such as the word *zoognick*—never before encountered because it was just created—and test whether observers acquire it. Other forms of learning, including operant conditioning, also are studied by using novel responses rather than by assessing past performances which would require monitoring every action that an organism has ever made both within and outside the experimental situation. Gewirtz's position with regard to observational learning is somewhat indeterminate because he alternately questions whether the phenomenon exists, reduces it to social facilitation of learned responses, and offers new descriptive labels (for example, "generalized imitation," "learn-to-learn," and "discriminated-operant") as explanations. To say that people learn by observation because they have "learned-to-learn," or because they have acquired a "complex discriminated-operant" in no way explains how responses are organized to form new observed patterns without reinforced performance.

Affective-Feedback Theories

Mowrer (1960) developed a sensory-feedback theory of imitation that emphasizes classical conditioning of positive and negative emotions evoked by reinforcement to stimuli arising from matching behavior. He distinguishes two forms of imitative learning in terms of whether the observer is reinforced directly or vicariously. In the first case, the model performs a response and at the same time rewards the observer. Through repeated contiguous association of the model's behavior with rewarding experiences, his responses eventually take on positive value for the observer. Through stimulus generalization, the observer can later produce self-rewarding experiences simply by performing the model's positively valenced behavior.

In the second "empathetic" form of imitative learning, the model not only exhibits the response, but also experiences the reinforcing consequences. It is assumed that the observer experiences the sensory concomitants of the model's behavior empathetically and intuits his satisfactions or discomforts. As a result of this empathetic conditioning, the observer is predisposed to reproduce the matching responses for the attendant positive sensory feedback.

There is substantial evidence (Bandura & Huston, 1961; Grusec, 1966; Henker, 1964; Mischel & Grusec, 1966; Mussen & Parker, 1965) that modeling can be augmented by increasing the positive qualities of a model or by having the observer witness the model being rewarded. These same studies, however, contain some contradictory findings with regard to the affective conditioning theory. Even though a model's rewarding qualities are equally associated with the different types of behaviors he performs, modeling affects tend to be specific rather than general. That is, model nurturance enhances imitation of some responses, has no effect upon others, and may actually diminish the adoption of still others (Bandura, Grusec, & Menlove, 1967a). A preliminary study by Foss (1964), in which mynas were taught unusual whistles played on a tape recorder, also failed to confirm the proposition that modeling is enhanced through positive conditioning. Sounds were imitated to the same extent regardless of whether they were presented alone or played only when the birds were being fed.

Mowrer's analysis of imitation is principally concerned with how modeled responses can be invested with positive or negative emotional qualities. Modeling theory, on the other hand, is more often called upon to explain the mechanics of acquisition of patterned behavior observationally rather than its emotional concomitants. A comprehensive theory must therefore elucidate how new patterns of behavior are constructed and the processes governing their execution.

In an elaboration of the affective-feedback theory of imitation, Aronfreed (1969) advanced the view that pleasurable and aversive affective states become conditioned to both response-produced stimuli and cognitive templates of modeled actions.

Imitative performances are presumed to be controlled by affective feedback from intentions as well as from proprioceptive cues generated during an overt act. This conceptualization of imitation is difficult to verify empirically because it does not specify in sufficient detail the characteristics of templates, the process whereby cognitive templates are acquired, the manner in which affective valences become coupled to templates, and how the emotion-arousing properties of templates are transferred to intentions and to proprioceptive cues intrinsic to overt responses. There is some experimental evidence, however, that has important implications for the basic assumptions contained in the notion of feedback.

Feedback theories, particularly those that attribute controlling functions to proprioceptive cues, are seriously challenged by the findings of curare-conditioning experiments in which animals are skeletally immobilized by the drug during aversive conditioning or extinction. These studies (Black, 1958; Black, Carlson, & Solomon, 1962; Solomon & Turner, 1962) demonstrate that learning can occur in the absence of skeletal responding and its correlated proprioceptive feedback. Results of deafferentation studies (Taub, Bacon, & Berman, 1965; Taub et al., 1966) also show that responses can be acquired, performed discriminatively, and extinguished with sensory somatic feedback surgically abolished by limb deafferentation. It would seem from these findings that the acquisition, integration, facilitation and inhibition of responses can be achieved through central mechanisms independent of peripheral sensory feedback.

It is also evident that rapid selection of responses from among a varied array of alternatives cannot be governed by sensory feedback since relatively few responses could be activated even incipiently during the brief time that people usually have to decide how to respond to the situations confronting them (Miller, 1964). Recognizing this problem, Mowrer (1960) has conjectured that the initial scanning and selection of responses occurs primarily at the cognitive rather than at the action level. Consistent with this view, in the social learning analysis of self-regulatory systems (Bandura, 1971a; 1971c) human behavior is largely controlled by anticipated consequences of prospective actions.

Human functioning would be exceedingly inflexible and unadaptive if responsiveness were controlled by affectivity in the behavior itself. Considering the highly discriminative character of social responsiveness, it is extremely doubtful that actions are regulated by affective qualities implanted in behavior. Aggression will serve as an example.

Hitting responses directed toward parents, peers, and inanimate objects differ little, if at all. Nevertheless, hitting parents is generally strongly inhibited, whereas physical aggression toward peers is freely expressed (Bandura, 1960; Bandura & Walters, 1959). Moreover, in certain well-defined contexts, particularly in competitive physical contact sports such as boxing, people will readily display vigorous physical aggression. One can more accurately predict the expression or inhibition of identical aggressive responses from knowledge of the social context (church or athletic gymnasium), the target (parent, priest, policeman, or peer), and other cues that reliably signify potential consequences, than from assessment of the affective value of aggressive behavior per se. It has been amply demonstrated (Bandura, 1971a) that selection and performance of matching responses is mainly governed by anticipated outcomes based on previous consequences that were either directly encountered, vicariously experienced, or self-administered. In other words, responses are chosen from available alternatives more often on the basis of their functional than their emotional value.

Affective feedback conceptions of modeling also fail to account for matching behavior when neither the model nor the observer is reinforced. In these instances, the theory can be preserved only by attributing inherent emotional properties to the behavior that may not always be warranted. In fact, a vast majority of the responses that are acquired observationally are not affectively valenced. This is exemplified by studies of observational learning of mechanical assembly tasks from filmed demonstrations that do not contain stimuli that would arouse the emotion essential for affective conditioning (Sheffield & Maccoby, 1961). Mowrer has, of course, pointed out that sensory experiences can also produce conditioned sensations or images. In most cases of observational learning imaginal or other symbolic representations of modeling stimuli may be the only important mediating processes. Sensory-feedback theories of imitation may therefore be primarily applicable to instances in which modeled responses incur relatively potent consequences so that observers come to anticipate similar emotional consequences if they were to imitate the behavior. Affective conditioning should therefore be regarded as a facilitative rather than a necessary condition for modeling.

Social Learning Theory

Most contemporary interpretations of learning assign a more prominent role to cognitive functioning in the acquisition and regulation of human behavior than did previous explanatory systems. Social learning theory (Bandura, 1969a; 1971c) assumes that modeling influences operate principally through their informative function, and that observers acquire mainly symbolic representations of modeled events rather than specific stimulus-response associations. In this formulation, modeling phenomena are governed by four interrelated subprocesses. These four subsystems are briefly discussed in the sections that follow.

ATTENTIONAL PROCESSES

One of the main component functions in observational learning involves attentional processes. Simply exposing persons to modeled responses does not in itself guarantee that they will attend closely to them, select from the total stimulus complex the most relevant events, and perceive accurately the cues to which their attention has been directed. An observer will fail to acquire matching behavior at the sensory registration level if he does not attend to, recognize, and differentiate the distinctive features of the model's responses. Discriminative observation is therefore one of the requisite conditions for observational learning.

A number of attention-controlling variables can be influential in determining which models are closely observed and which are ignored. The incentives provided for learning modeled behavior, the motivational and psychological characteristics of the observer, and the physical and acquired distinctiveness of the model as well as his power and interpersonal attractiveness are some of the many factors that exert selective control over the attention people pay to the variety of modeled activities they encounter in their everyday life. The people with whom one regularly associates delimit the types of behavior that one will repeatedly observe and hence learn most thoroughly.

RETENTION PROCESSES

A second basic component function in observational learning that has been virtually ignored in theories of imitation is the retention of modeled events. When a person observes a model's behavior without performing the responses, he can acquire the modeled responses while they are occurring only in representational form. In order to reproduce this behavior without the continued presence of external modeling cues, he must retain the original observational inputs in some symbolic form. This is a particularly interesting problem in the instance of observationally acquired response patterns that are retained over extended periods, though rarely, if ever, activated into overt performance until attainment of an age or social status at which the activity is considered appropriate.

Observational learning involves two representational systems, the imaginal and the verbal. During exposure, modeling stimuli produce through a process of sensory conditioning relatively enduring, retrievable images of modeled sequences of behavior. Indeed, when stimulus events are highly correlated, as when a name is consistently associated with a given person, it is virtually impossible to hear the name without experiencing imagery of the person's physical characteristics. Similarly, reference to activities (for example, golfing or surfing), places (San Francisco, New York, Paris), and things (the Washington Monument, an airliner) that one has previously observed immediately elicits vivid imaginal representations of the absent physical stimuli.

The second representational system, which probably accounts for the notable speed of observational learning and long-term retention of modeled contents by humans, involves verbal coding of observed events. Most of the cognitive processes that regulate behavior are primarily verbal rather than visual. To take a simple example, the route traversed by a model can be acquired, retained, and later reproduced more accurately by verbal coding of the visual information into a sequence of right-left turns (RRLRR) than by reliance upon visual imagery of the itinerary. Observational learning and retention are facilitated by such codes because they carry a great deal of information in an easily stored form. After modeled responses have been transformed into images and readily utilizable verbal symbols, these memory codes serve as guides for subsequent reproduction of matching responses.

The influential role of symbolic representation in observational learning is supported in several studies differing in age of subjects and in content of modeled activities. In one experiment (Bandura, Grusec, & Menlove, 1966) children observed several complex sequences of behavior modeled on film. During exposure the children either watched attentively, coded the novel responses into their verbal equivalents as they were performed by the model, or counted rapidly while watching the film to prevent implicit verbal coding of modeling stimuli. A subsequent test of observational learning disclosed that children who verbally coded the modeled patterns reproduced significantly more matching responses than those in the viewing-along condition, who in turn showed a higher level of acquisition than children who engaged in competing symbolization. Children within the verbalizing condition reproduced a high proportion (60%) of the modeled responses that they had coded into words, whereas they retrieved a low proportion (25%) of the responses they failed to code.

Coates and Hartup (1969) investigated developmental changes in the role of verbal coding of modeling stimuli in observational learning within the context of the production deficiency hypothesis. According to this hypothesis, which was originally proposed by Keeney,Cannizzo and Flavell (1967), young children are capable of but do not utilize symbolic activities that would facilitate performance, whereas older children spontaneously produce and employ verbal mediators, and therefore do not benefit from further prompts to engage in symbolic activities. Consistent with this view, Coates and Hartup found that induced verbal labeling of modeling stimuli enhanced observational learning in young children but had no effect on older subjects. The issue requires further study in view of further evidence that induced verbal coding can facilitate observational learning in both older children (Bandura, Grusec & Menlove, 1966) and adults (Bandura & Jeffery, 1971; Gerst, 1971). Moreover, van Hekken (1969) found that it was the older children who spontaneously used symbolic skills in other learning tasks rather than the "nonmediators" who achieved increases in observational learning through induced verbal coding of modeling stimuli.

Additional evidence for the influence of symbolic coding operations in the acquisition and retention of modeled responses is furnished by Gerst (1971). College students observed a filmed model perform complex motor responses composed of intricate movements taken from the alphabet of the deaf. Immediately after observing each modeled response, subjects engaged in one of four symbolic activities for a period of one minute. One group reinstated the response through vivid imagery; a second group coded the modeling stimuli into concrete verbal terms by describing the specific response elements and their movements; the third group generated concise labels that incorporated the essential ingredients of the responses. (For example, a pretzel-shaped response might be labeled as an orchestra conductor moving his baton in a symphonic finale.) Subjects assigned to the control group performed mental calculations to impede symbolic coding of the depicted events. The subjects reproduced the modeled responses immediately after coding, and following a 15-minute period during which they performed a distracting task designed to prevent symbolic rehearsal of modeled responses.

All three coding operations enhanced observational learning. Concise labeling and imaginal codes were equally effective in aiding immediate reproduction of modeled responses, both being superior to the concrete verbal form. The delayed test for retention of matching responses showed concise labeling to be the best coding system for memory representation. Subjects in this condition retained significantly more matching responses than those who relied upon imagery and concrete verbalizations.

The relative superiority of the summary labeling code is shown even more clearly when matching performances are scored according to a stringent criterion requiring that all response elements be reproduced in the exact sequence in which they were originally modeled. Subjects who coded the modeling stimuli with concise labels were able to reproduce approximately twice as many well-integrated responses in the retention test as the other groups. Moreover, modeled responses for which subjects retained the summary codes were reproduced at a higher level of accuracy (52%), than those for which the code was lost (7%).

In a recent paper, Gewirtz and Stingle (1968) questioned the value of theories of modeling that include symbolic processes on the grounds that the symbolic events are inferred from the matching behavior they are designed to explain. This type of criticism might apply to theories that attribute behavior to hypothetical internal agencies having only a tenuous relationship to antecedent events and to the behavior that they supposedly explain. In the experiments cited here, symbolic events are independently manipulated and not simply inferred from matching behavior.

Before discussing other factors that facilitate retention of symbolically modeled contents, the structural characteristics of representation should be clarified. Internal representations are not necessarily exact replicas of external modeling stimuli. Indeed, the changes that could be produced through modeling influences would be limited if coded representations were always structurally isomorphic to individual responses performed by others. Relevant evidence will be cited later to show that observers often abstract common features from a variety of modeled responses and construct higher-order codes that have wide generality. Moreover, results reported by Gerst (1971) indicate that modeled behavior is most effectively acquired and retained when modeled configurations are likened to events that are familiar and meaningful to the observer. These findings accord with the common observation that learning through modeling is often enhanced when required performances are represented as resembling familiar activities. The members of a ski class that could not learn to transfer their weight to the downhill ski despite several demonstrations by the instructor were observed to promptly master the maneuver when asked to ski as though they were pointing a serving tray downhill throughout the turns and traverses.

In social learning theory observers function as active agents who transform, classify, and organize modeling stimuli into easily remembered schemes rather than as quiescent cameras or tape recorders that simply store isomorphic representations of modeled events.

Another means of stabilizing and strengthening acquired responses is rehearsal operations. The level of observational learning can be considerably enhanced through practice or overt rehearsal of modeled response sequences, particularly if the rehearsal is interposed after natural segments of a larger modeled pattern. Of greater import is evidence that covert rehearsal, which can be readily engaged in when overt participation is either impeded or impracticable, may likewise increase retention of acquired matching behavior (Bandura & Jeffery, 1971; Michael & Maccoby, 1961). Like coding, rehearsal involves active processes.

There is reason to believe that the benefits accruing from rehearsal result from an individual's reorganization and recoding of input events rather than from sheer repetition.

MOTORIC REPRODUCTION PROCESSES

The third major component of modeling phenomena is concerned with motoric reproduction processes. This involves the utilization of symbolic representations of modeled patterns to guide overt performances. The process of representational guidance is similar to response execution under conditions in which a person follows an externally depicted pattern, or is directed through a series of instructions to enact novel response sequences. The only difference is that a directed performance is guided by external cues, whereas in delayed modeling, behavioral reproduction is monitored by symbolic counterparts of absent stimuli.

The rate and level of observational learning will be partly governed, at the motoric level, by the availability of essential component responses. Complex modes of behavior are produced by combinations of previously learned components which may in themselves be relatively complicated compounds. In instances where observers lack some of the necessary components, the constituent elements may be modeled first; then in stepwise fashion, increasingly intricate compounds can be developed imitatively.

REINFORCEMENT AND MOTIVATIONAL PROCESSES

The final component function concerns motivational or reinforcement processes. A person may acquire and retain the capability of skillful execution of modeled behavior, but the learning will rarely be activated into overt performance if negative sanctions or unfavorable incentive conditions obtain. In such circumstances, the introduction of positive incentives promptly translates observational learning into action (Bandura, 1965b). Reinforcement variables not only regulate the overt expression of matching behavior, but they can also affect observational learning by exerting selective control over the types of modeled events to which people are most likely to attend. Further, they facilitate selective retention by activating deliberate coding and rehearsal of modeled behaviors that have functional value. These and other issues bearing on the role of reinforcement in modeling are discussed more fully in subsequent sections.

If one is merely interested in producing imitative behavior, some of the subprocesses outlined above can be disregarded. A model who repeatedly demonstrates desired responses, instructs others to reproduce them, manually prompts the behavior when it fails to occur, and offers valued rewards for correct imitations, will eventually elicit matching responses in most people. It may require 1, 10, or 100 demonstration trials, but if one persists, the desired behavior will eventually be evoked. If, on the other hand, one wishes to explain the conditions governing modeling phenomena, a diverse set of controlling variables must be considered. The critical subprocesses and their determinants are summarized in the following chart.

Theories of imitation that disregard cognitive functioning cannot adequately account for variations in matching performances that result from symbolic activities (Bandura & Jeffery, 1971; Gerst, 1971) when modeling stimuli and reinforcement contingencies remain the same for all subjects. Nor can such differences be attributed to prior history of reinforcement since there is no reason to believe that subjects randomly assigned to a symbolic coding condition have been more often rewarded for imitation than those not induced to code modeled events into words or images. The limitations of conceptual schemes that depict matching behavior as controlled solely by external stimuli and reinforcing consequences are also readily apparent in instances of repeated presentation of modeling stimuli under favorable reinforcement conditions that fail to produce matching responses. The difficulties encountered by Lovaas in creating imitative behavior in some autistic children have stimulated research

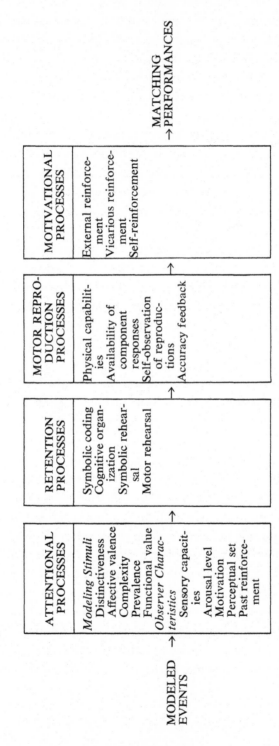

Subprocesses in the social learning view of observational learning.

on attentional deficits (Lovaas, Rehm & Schreibman, 1969). Preliminary findings indicate that autistic children have difficulty in processing information conveyed through different sensory modalities. However, their rate of learning is greatly facilitated by various attention-enhancing procedures (Wasserman, 1969) that would undoubtedly improve observational learning. Given evidence that observers often fail to remember what they have learned, nonmediational theories will eventually be forced to consider retention processes as well.

In any given instance, absence of appropriate matching behavior following exposure to modeling stimuli may result from failures in sensory registration of modeled events, inadequate coding of modeling stimuli for memory representation, retention decrements, motoric deficiencies, or unwillingness to perform matching behavior because of inadequate reinforcement. For these reasons theories which contend that people imitate because they have been intermittently reinforced for imitating in the past may have limited explanatory power.

Other theorists have proposed interpretations of imitation in which representational processes, in one form or another, figure prominently. In Sheffield's view (1961), matching performances are mediated by perceptual representations of modeled events, mainly in the form of visual imagery. These perceptual responses, or "blueprints," which serve as cues for overt action, are assumed to be conditioned solely through contiguous association with stimulus events.

This conceptualization and social learning have some points of similarity. Both positions postulate a representational guidance system for matching behavior which can be established without overt responding. But they differ in several important respects. In the social learning view, modeling stimuli serve more as sources of information than as automatic conditioners; observers often perform operations on modeling inputs so that transformational and organizational processes are involved as well as associational ones; less structural correspondence is assumed between memory codes and the original modeled patterns; verbal representation is assigned a greater response guidance function;

and reinforcement, which receives no mention in Sheffield's formulation, is treated in social learning as a factor that can facilitate observational learning.

Piaget's Theory

Piaget (1951) presents a developmental account of imitation in which symbolic representation assumes an important function, especially in higher forms of modeling. At the earlier sensorimotor stages of development, imitative responding can be evoked only by having the model repeat the child's immediately preceding responses in alternating imitative sequences. During this period, according to Piaget, the child is unable to imitate responses that he has not previously performed spontaneously because actions cannot be assimilated unless they correspond to already existing schemas. Piaget reports that when models introduce new behavioral elements or even familiar responses that children have acquired but are not exhibiting at the moment, they do not respond imitatively. Imitation is thus restricted to reproduction of activities that children have already developed, that they can see themselves make, and that they have performed immediately before the model's reiteration.

If the above observations based on Piaget's longitudinal study of his own three children are replicable, then young children have weaker capabilities for observational learning than subhuman species. Animals (Adler & Adler, 1968) and birds (Foss, 1964) can learn new patterns of behavior observationally, and modeling stimuli can acquire the capacity to evoke existing matching responses even though the organism was not performing them beforehand. It is assumed by Piaget that during initial stages children do not distinguish between self-imitation and imitation of the actions of others. If this is the case, then the theory must explain why a child's own behavior can originally induce matching responses but identical actions initiated by others cannot.

In Piaget's view, schemas, which refer to schematic outlines of activities, determine what behaviors can or cannot be imitated. Unfortunately, the descriptive account does not specify in any detail the extent to which schemas are learned or furnished innately and, if learned, the process whereby general features of an activity are abstracted from otherwise different instances. From the perspective of the multiprocess theory of modeling, deficiencies in imitative performance, which are typically attributed by Piaget to insufficiently differentiated schemas, may likewise result from inadequate observation of modeling stimuli, from motoric difficulties in executing learned patterns, or from faulty reinforcement. The latter factor deserves further comment because of its important bearing on evaluation of findings from naturalistic studies of modeling.

Observational data must be accepted with reservation when the model's reactions to the child's performances are not reported. Lovaas (1967) has shown that young children imitate precisely when they are rewarded only for exact matches, but if they are positively reinforced without regard to the quality of their reproduction, their imitations deteriorate rapidly. When only the child's responses are observed and recorded, imitative deficiencies arising from faulty reinforcement are likely to be erroneously attributed to his shortcomings. Since observational studies of the type conducted by Piaget involve a two-way influence process, imitative performances reflect not only the competency of the child but the reactions of the participating model to accurate and inadequate matches. If models respond alike to performances that differ widely in quality, children will tend to disregard modeling stimuli, whereas they reproduce accurately any activities within their capacity if models respond discriminately.

The discussion thus far has been concerned with early stages in the development of imitation as depicted by Piaget. As a child's intellectual development progresses, he becomes capable of delayed imitation of modeled events which he cannot see himself make. These changes presumably come about through coordination of visual and sensorimotor schemas, and differentiation of the child's own actions from those of others. He now begins systematic trial-and-error performance of responses until he achieves good matches to new modeled patterns.

At the final stages of development, which generally begin in the second year of life, children attain representative imitation. Schemas are coordinated internally to form new and complex patterns of modeled behavior without requiring overt provisional trials of actions. This covert imitation occurs through imaginal representation of modeled performances, which also serves as the basis for reproducing matching behavior when models are no longer present. Had Piaget extended his studies of imitation into later childhood years, it is likely that verbal representation would also have emerged as an important functional mediator in delayed modeling.

A comprehensive theory of modeling must explain not only how patterned behavior is acquired observationally, but also when and how frequently imitative behavior will be performed, the persons toward whom it will be expressed, and the social settings in which it is most likely to be exhibited. Piaget's account of imitation contains only a few passing remarks about the motivational factors regulating performance of matching behavior. Imitation is variously attributed to an intrinsic need for acting and knowing, to a desire to reproduce actions that differ partially from existing schemas, and to the esteem in which the model is held. Most researchers in the field of modeling would regard these factors as much too general to account satisfactorily for the highly discriminative character of imitative responding. In view of the abundant evidence that imitative performances can be strongly controlled by their external consequences, the influence of reinforcement variables must be considered in explanatory schemes, whatever their orientation may be.

CONTROVERSIAL ISSUES IN MODELING

Several controversial issues in the field of modeling were alluded to in the preceding review of theories formulated to explain imitative processes. In the present section the major points in dispute are discussed more fully. It should be noted here that since modeling depends on basic psychological subprocesses, such as attention, cognitive functioning, and retention, some of the issues are by no means unique to this phenomenon.

Criteria of Observational Learning

There has been some debate concerning the criteria used for identifying the occurrence of observational learning. Learning may be reflected either in associational or in organizational changes in performance. In the former case, people learn to respond to certain situations in a particular way. As a result of correlated experiences existing forms of behavior are brought under the control of stimuli to which individuals previously did not respond at all, or reacted in a substantially different manner. They learn, for example, to stop at red signal lights, to avoid certain places and things with which they have had painful experiences, to perform activities that are encouraged and rewarded in particular settings, and to react emotionally to specific sounds and sights. Here learning is defined in terms of changes in stimulus control rather than in the characteristics of the behavior itself.

The second way in which learning is indexed, which has received much greater attention in modeling research, involves organization of response components into new forms of patterned behavior. To take a simple example: Persons can produce a variety of elementary sounds as part of their natural endowment. By combining existing sounds one can create a novel and exceedingly complex verbal response such as *supercalifragilistic-expialidocious.*

Some writers (Aronfreed, 1969; Patterson, Littman & Bricker, 1967) have questioned whether behavior formed through unique combinations of available elements represents learning since the components already exist in the subject's repertoire. According to this line of reasoning, a pianist who has mastered a Beethoven piano concerto has learned nothing new because all the finger movements already existed in his repertoire; and Beethoven cannot be credited with creating new symphonic music since he simply rearranged a few preexisting notes.

Response novelty is defined in terms of empirical criteria rather than a priori estimations. Any behavior that has an extremely low or zero probability of occurrence given appropriate stimulus conditions qualifies as a novel response. Most new compound responses are composed of common behavioral elements.

It was previously noted that modeling influences, depending on their nature, can have three quite different effects on observers. Disputes over observational learning sometimes result from failure to distinguish modeling experiments designed primarily to produce learning effects from those intended to elucidate inhibitory or social facilitation effects. Observational response learning is most convincingly demonstrated in studies employing specially constructed unique responses. It is extremely improbable, for example, that neologisms such as *lickitstickit* or *wetosmacko* (Bandura, Ross, & Ross, 1963a) would ever be uttered by subjects during an investigator's lifetime if these verbal responses were never modeled.

The establishment of new stimulus control of behavior through modeling is well illustrated by experiments in which observers learn to respond emotionally to previously neutral stimuli as a result of seeing others suffer painful experiences when the stimuli appear (Berger, 1962; Bandura & Rosenthal, 1966; Craig & Weinstein, 1965). Instrumental responding can similarly be brought under new stimulus control as a result of observing behavior of others that is rewarded whenever certain stimuli are present and ignored or punished when performed in other contexts (McDavid, 1962, 1964; Wilson, 1958).

Some researchers (Gewirtz & Stingle, 1968) have concerned themselves particularly with the appearance of first imitative responses on the assumption that they help to explain subsequent observational learning. According to these authors, initial imitative responses may emerge by chance, through physical guidance, or be gradually shaped by differential reinforcement of randomly emitted behavior. These imitations are presumably strengthened through direct reinforcement. Eventually response similarity becomes a discriminative stimulus signifying probable consequences and intermittent external reinforcement of matching behavior produces generalized imitation of different models in diverse situations even though such behavior is not always rewarded.

There is some reason to question whether conditions governing initial imitations necessarily explain subsequent observational learning. Modeling phenomena are by no means equivalent at different periods of development; consequently, the determinants of early imitations may provide an insufficient or even a misleading explanation of how modeled responses are later acquired.

In early years imitative responses are evoked directly by a model's actions, but in later periods matching behavior is typically performed long after exposure to modeling stimuli and in the absence of the model. Immediate imitation does not require much in the way of symbolic functioning because the behavioral reproduction is externally guided by the model's performance. By contrast, in delayed imitation the absent modeled events must be internally represented in symbolic form, and covert rehearsal and organizational processes that facilitate long-term retention of acquired contents emerge as important determinants of observational learning.

There is no doubt that rewarding imitative gestures, vocalizations, and social responses in young children will increase their willingness to adopt behavior displayed by others. However, prior intermittent reinforcement of matching responses in no way explains why people who transform modeling stimuli into easily remembered verbal schemes achieve better acquisition and retention of modeled responses than those who do not verbally code the external behavioral events for memory representation (Bandura & Jeffery, 1971; Gerst, 1971). Under these types of conditions, variations in modeling are accounted for by cognitive functions rather than by past history of reinforcement.

Given the importance of cognitive functioning in observational learning, the experimental paradigm regularly employed in operant conditioning studies of imitation may be poorly suited to its elucidation. In the standard procedure a model exhibits discrete responses which observers copy either during or immediately after demonstration. Instantaneous matching can occur without much symbolic representation or learning for that matter, just as individuals can successfully assemble a complicated apparatus by following a continually accessible set of directions, yet be unable to produce the correct performances when the external aids are removed. The difference between physically prompted and delayed imitation is analogous to the difference between drawing a picture of one's automobile when it is at hand, and from memory. In the latter situation, the hand does not automatically sketch the car; rather one must rely on memory guides, mainly in the form of mental images.

Exposure to modeled performances often fails to produce matching behavior in observers. When this occurs in young children who have been explicitly instructed to reproduce demonstrated activities, the children are often characterized as lacking an "imitative repertoire." Imitative behavior is defined in terms of its similarity to a modeled pattern rather than as a specific set of responses, and hence it may take a variety of forms. It is therefore unclear what an "imitative repertoire," which implies a specific collection of contents, would represent. As previously noted, people may fail to imitate behavior within their capabilities for a number of reasons. They may lack requisite components, or they may be capable of but unwilling to perform the desired behavior. In an experiment reported by Bandura and Barab (1971), grossly retarded children who had displayed no matching behavior even when actively encouraged to do so promptly imitated every modeled response when rewards were changed and when a familiar person demonstrated the behavior. These findings, together with data cited earlier, indicate a need for caution in attributing deficiencies in imitative performance to deficits in imitative learning.

Scope of Modeling Influences

It is widely assumed that imitation can produce at best mimicry of specific responses exhibited by others. There are several reasons why such limited learning effects are ascribed to imitation. The term carries a strong connotation that the process is confined to literal copying of particular modeled responses. Formal definitions of imitation do not specify which properties of the model's behavior are adopted. Some investigators have therefore concluded that the phenomenon applies only to matching of simple physical characteristics. The behavior displayed by others ordinarily varies on a number of stimulus dimensions which differ in content, complexity, and discriminability. It is arbitrary which modeled attributes are selected as relevant in any given experiment. Although the matching process frequently involves reproduction of concrete patterns of behavior, in many instances observers must match subtle features common to a variety of modeled responses that differ on several other attributes.

Another factor that contributed to underestimation of the scope of modeling influences was the widespread use of a restricted experimental paradigm. In these studies a model performs a few responses designated by a single prominent feature and observers are subsequently tested for precise reproduction of the modeled behavior in identical or similar situations. Under these circumscribed conditions, experiments could yield only mimicry of specific responses. This led many researchers to place severe limitations on the behavioral changes that can be attributed to modeling influences.

In order to demonstrate that limitations ascribed to modeling were inherent in the methodology rather than in the phenomenon itself, several experiments were conducted (Bandura & Harris, 1966; Bandura & McDonald, 1963; Bandura & Mischel, 1965) requiring a more complex form of modeling. These studies utilized a paradigm in which persons observed models responding consistently to diverse stimuli in accordance with a

pre-selected rule. Tests for generalized imitation were later conducted by different experimenters, in different social contexts
with the models absent, and with different stimulus items. The
results disclosed that observers respond to new situations in a
style that is consistent with the models' dispositions without ever
having observed the models responding to these particular stimuli.

In this higher-order form of modeling the performer's behavior conveys information to observers about the characteristics of
appropriate responses. Observers must abstract common attributes exemplified in diverse modeled responses and formulate a
rule for generating similar patterns of behavior. Responses performed by subjects that embody the observationally derived rule
are likely to resemble the behavior that the model would be inclined to exhibit under similar circumstances, even though subjects had never witnessed the model's behavior in these new situations.

Evidence that response-generative rules can be acquired observationally has interesting implications for controversies regarding language learning. Because of the highly generative
character of linguistic behavior it has commonly been assumed
by psycholinguists (Brown & Bellugi, 1964; Ervin, 1964; Menyuk, 1964) that imitation cannot play much part in language development and production. This conclusion is largely based on
the mistaken assumption that one can learn through observation
only the concrete features of behavior, not its abstract properties.
Obviously children are able to construct an almost infinite variety of sentences that they have never heard. Therefore, rather
than acquiring specific utterances through imitation, children
must learn sets of rules on the basis of which they can generate
an unlimited number of novel grammatical sentences. The importance of imitative learning in language development was further discounted on the grounds that children often display only
crude approximations of adult verbalizations (Brown & Bellugi,
1964), and they can acquire linguistic rules without engaging in
any motor speech (Lenneberg, 1967).

The above criticisms have validity when applied to theories of imitation that emphasize verbatim repetition of modeled responses and that assume matching responses must be performed and reinforced in order to be learned. It is evident from the material already discussed at length that the social learning interpretation of modeling processes is compatible with rule-learning theories advanced by psycholinguists. Both points of view assign special importance to the abstraction of productive rules from diverse modeled examples. The differentiation made by psycholinguists between language competence and language performance corresponds to the distinction made between learning and performance in social learning theory. Another point of similarity is that neither approach assumes that observational learning necessitates performance. Finally, the basic rules, or prototypes, that guide production of grammatical utterances are presumed to be extracted from individual modeled instances rather than innately programmed. People are innately equipped with information-processing capacities, not with response-productive rules.

Rules about grammatical relations between words cannot be learned unless they are exemplified in the verbal behavior of models. A number of experiments have been conducted to discover conditions that facilitate abstraction of rules from verbal modeling cues. The principle underlying a model's varied responses can be most readily discerned if its identifying characteristics are distinctly repeated in responses which differ in other aspects. If, for example, one were to place a series of objects first on tables, then on chairs, boxes, and other things, simultaneously verbalizing the common prepositional relationship between these different objects, a child would eventually discern the grammatical principle. He could then easily generate a novel grammatical sentence if a toy hippopotamus were placed on a xylophone and the child were asked to describe the stimulus event enacted.

Changes in linguistic behavior are difficult to achieve because sentences represent complex stimulus patterns in which the identifying features of syntactic structure cannot be easily discerned.

The influential role of both modeling and discrimination processes in language development is revealed in an experiment designed to alter the syntactic style of young children who had no formal grammatical knowledge of the linguistic features selected for modification (Bandura & Harris, 1966). Children increased grammatical constructions in accord with the rules guiding the modeled utterances when verbal modeling influences were combined with attention-directing and reinforcement procedures designed to increase syntactic discriminability. This finding was replicated by Odom, Liebert, and Hill (1968) and extended by Rosenthal and his associates (Carroll, Rosenthal, & Brysh, 1969; Rosenthal & Whitebook, 1970), who demonstrated that exposure to verbal modeling altered structural and tense components of children's linguistic behavior congruent with the model's sentence rules.

The studies cited above were principally devoted to the modification of linguistic features with which the children had some familiarity. A recent study by Liebert, Odom, Hill, and Huff (1969) has shown that children can acquire through modeling an arbitrary ungrammatical rule, which they use to generate peculiar sentences.

Further evidence for the influential role of modeling processes in language acquisition is provided by naturalistic studies employing sequential analyses of children's verbalizations and the immediately following parental responses. Such studies disclose that young children's speech is at best semi-grammatical; in approximately 30 percent of instances adults repeat children's verbalizations in a grammatically more complex form, accenting the elements that may have been omitted and inaccurately employed (Brown & Bellugi, 1964); and children often reproduce the more complicated grammatical reconstructions modeled by adults (Slobin, 1968). Of special interest is evidence (Lovaas, 1967) that the accuracy of children's imitations is subject to reinforcement control. That is, when rewards are contingent on correct reproduction of modeled responses, children display precise imitativeness. On the other hand, when children can gain rewards irrespective of the accuracy with which they reproduce modeled utterances, the fidelity of their matching responses deteriorates.

Additional illustrations of how behavior-guiding principles can be transmitted through modeling are provided in experiments designed to modify moral judgmental orientations (Bandura & McDonald, 1963; Cowan, Langer, Heavenrich, & Nathanson, 1969; Le Furgy & Woloshin, 1969); delay of gratification patterns (Bandura & Mischel; 1965; Stumphauzer, 1969); and styles of information-seeking (Rosenthal, Zimmerman, & Durning, 1970). Researchers have also begun to study how modeling influences alter cognitive functioning of the type described by Piaget and his followers. Some of these studies are concerned with the principle of conservation, which reflects a child's ability to recognize that a given property remains invariant despite external changes that make it look different (as when the same amount of liquid is poured into different shaped containers.) Young children who do not conserve are able to do so consistently as a result of observing a model's conservation judgments and supporting explanations (Rosenthal & Zimmerman, 1970). Moreover, conservation judgments induced through modeling generalize to new characteristics; they endure over time; and they do not differ from conservation concepts acquired by children in the course of their everyday experiences (Sullivan, 1967).

The broader effects of modeling influences are further revealed in experimental paradigms employing multiple models who display diverse patterns of behavior. Contrary to common belief, it is possible to create novel modes of response solely through imitation (Bandura, Ross, & Ross, 1963a). When individuals are exposed to a variety of models, they may select one or more of them as primary sources of behavior; but rarely do they confine their imitation to a single source, nor do they reproduce all of the characteristics of the preferred model. Rather, observers generally exhibit relatively novel responses representing amalgams of the behavior of different models. The particular admixtures of behavioral elements vary from person to person.

Within a given family even same-sex siblings may thus develop unlike personality characters as a result of imitating different combinations of parental and sibling attributes. A succession of modeling influences in which observers later became sources of behavior for new members would most likely produce a gradual imitative evolution of novel patterns bearing little resemblance to those exhibited by the original models.

The degree of behavioral innovation that can be achieved through imitation will depend on the diversity of modeled patterns. In homogeneous cultures in which all models display similar modes of response, imitative behavior may undergo little or no change across successive models, but model dissimilarity is apt to foster new divergent patterns. The evidence accumulated to date suggests that, depending on their complexity and diversity, modeling influences can produce, in addition to mimicry of specific responses, behavior that is generative and innovative in character.

Locus of Response Integration

Development of new modes of response requires organization of behavioral elements into certain patterns and sequences. Theories of imitation differ as to whether component responses are integrated into new forms mainly at central or at peripheral levels. Despite the importance of the issue, there has been relatively little research on this aspect of observational learning.

Classical conditioning theories of imitation do not address themselves at all to the issue of response acquisition. They are principally concerned with associative processes whereby existing response patterns are brought under the control of social stimuli and endowed with positive or negative emotion-arousing properties. Instrumental conditioning formulations (Baer & Sherman, 1964; Gewirtz & Stingle, 1968) assume that constituent response elements are selected from overt performances by the joint influence of discriminative stimuli and differential reinforcement; the extracted components are then sequentially chained to form more complex arrangements of behavior. Since it is assumed that behavior is organized into new patterns in the course of performance, learning requires overt responding and immediate reinforcement.

In social learning theory (Bandura, 1969a), it is assumed that behavior is learned and organized chiefly through central integrative mechanisms prior to motor execution. By observing a model of the desired behavior, an individual forms an idea of how response components must be combined and temporally sequenced to produce new behavioral configurations. In other words, patterned behavior is largely guided by symbolic representation rather than formed through reinforced performance.

Observational learning without performance is abundantly documented in modeling studies using a nonresponse acquisition procedure (Bandura, 1965a; Flanders, 1968). After observing models perform novel modes of response, subjects can describe the entire pattern of behavior with considerable accuracy, and they often achieve errorless behavioral reproductions on the first test trial. These findings indicate that modeled behavior is learned as a whole in symbolic form before behavioral enactment.

It is commonly believed that controversies about the locus of learning cannot be satisfactorily resolved because learning must be inferred from performance. This may very well be the case in experimentation with animals. To determine whether a rat has mastered a maze one must run him through it. With humans, there exists a reasonably accurate index of learning that is independent of motor performance. To measure whether a human has learned a maze by observing the successful performances of a model, one need only ask him to describe the correct pattern of right-left turns. Such an experiment would undoubtedly reveal that people can learn through modeling before they perform.

In many instances, of course, observational learning alone is not sufficient to produce faultless performances. There are several reasons for this. When modeled patterns are observed briefly or only sporadically, individuals generally acquire at best a fragmentary sketch of the demonstrated activities. Behavioral reproduction is defective because the guiding internal representation is inadequate. Overt practice helps to identify the aspects that were missed entirely or only partially learned. Given the opportunity to observe the same behavior again, individuals are likely to concentrate their attention on the problematic segment to fill in the missing guides required for accurate performance.

Even when clear symbolic representation of modeled activities is developed and retained, behavioral enactment may be faulty because individuals do not have the physical capabilities necessary for the activities. A young child can learn observationally the behavior for driving an automobile, but if he is too short to operate the controls, he will be unable to perform the set of responses needed to maneuver the vehicle successfully.

Accurate behavioral enactment of modeled events is also difficult to achieve under conditions where the model's performance is governed by subtle adjustment of internal responses that are unobservable and not easy to communicate verbally. An aspiring operatic singer may benefit considerably from observing an accomplished voice instructor; nevertheless, skilled vocal reproduction is hampered by the fact that the model's laryngeal and respiratory muscular responses are neither readily observable nor easily described verbally.

The problem of behavioral reproduction is further complicated in the case of highly coordinated motor skills such as golf, in which a person cannot see most of the responses that he is making, and must therefore rely primarily on proprioceptive feedback cues and verbal reports of onlookers. It is exceedingly difficult to guide actions that are not easily observed or to identify the corrective adjustments needed to achieve a close match of symbolic model and overt performance. To facilitate development of motor skills, delayed self-observation through videotape procedures is increasingly employed. In most everyday learning, people achieve rough approximations of desired behavior by observation; their initial behavioral enactments are then further refined through self-corrective adjustments on the basis of informative feedback from performance.

The Modeling Process and Transmission of Response Information

As previously noted, a major function of modeling stimuli is to transmit information to observers about how response elements must be organized to produce required patterns of behavior. This response information can be conveyed through physical demonstration, through pictorial representation, or through verbal description.

Much social learning occurs through casual or directed observation of performances by real-life models. Indeed, imitative learning in young children depends almost entirely upon behavioral modeling. As linguistic competence is acquired, verbal modeling is gradually substituted for behavioral modeling as the preferred model of response guidance. People are aided in assembling and operating complicated mechanical equipment, in acquiring social, vocational, and recreational skills, and in learning appropriate behavior for almost any situation by consulting the written descriptions in instructional manuals. Verbal forms of modeling are used extensively because one can transmit through words an almost infinite variety of behavioral patterns that would be exceedingly difficult and time-consuming to portray behaviorally. Moreover, since verbal description is an effective means of focusing attention on relevant aspects of ongoing activities, verbal modeling often accompanies behavioral demonstrations.

Another influential source of social learning at all age levels is the abundant and diverse symbolic modeling provided in television, films, and other audiovisual displays. There is a large body of research evidence (Bandura, 1969a; Flanders, 1968) demonstrating that both children and adults acquire attitudes, emotional responses, and complex patterns of behavior through exposure to pictorially presented models. In view of the efficacy of pictorial modeling and the large amount of time people spend watching televised productions, mass media may play an influential role in shaping behavior and social attitudes. With further developments in communication technology whereby any desired activity can be portrayed on request at any time on remote television consoles (Parker, 1970), parents, teachers, and other traditional role models may occupy less prominent roles in the social learning process as increasing use is made of symbolic modeling influences.

Response information can be transmitted, though less precisely, through modalities other than auditory and visual media. In learning to speak, deaf-blind persons rely on kinesthetic modeling by matching through touch the mouth and laryngeal muscular responses of verbalizing models (Keller, 1927; Young & Hawk, 1955).

Disputes have arisen in the literature because different labels are applied to these various modes of conveying response information. Some writers reserve the term "imitation" for instances in which observers reproduce responses which are demonstrated socially (Fouts & Parton, 1969), "copying" for mechanical demonstrations (Fouts & Parton, 1969), and "instructions" for verbal demonstrations (Masters & Branch, 1969). Others define copying as a special instance of imitation in which socially demonstrated behavior is precisely matched (Miller & Dollard, 1941). It would be advantageous to use diverse concepts if the changes produced through different information modes involve fundamentally different learning processes. If, on the other hand, they reflect essentially the same learning process, then arbitrary conceptual distinctions are more likely to obscure than to clarify the phenomenon.

Social learning theory (Bandura, 1969a) is more concerned with the process whereby representation of patterned activities serves a response guidance function than with the particular form in which response information is presented. It is assumed that the basic matching process is the same regardless of whether the desired behavior is conveyed through words, pictures, or actions.

Controversies emerge about the conditions considered to be essential for modeling when the phenomenon is defined in terms of how the requisite activities are portrayed. In several experiments Parton and his associates (Dubanoski & Parton, 1968; Fouts & Parton, 1969) compared the accuracy with which children placed objects in selected locations after observing a film in which object placements were made by a person in full view, by a hand, by moving the objects with nylon thread, or by a sweep of the camera depicting the objects alone and then in their appropriate locations. Not unexpectedly, comparable matching performances were obtained regardless of the mode of conveyance.

Human transmitters are widely employed in modeling experiments, not because this is the only means of response guidance, but because under conditions of everyday life response patterns are usually depicted, whether deliberately or inadvertently, through social demonstration. Moreover, in the case of most social behavior the model's actions are the critical events, and to remove the social model is to erase the behavior. How, for example, can one have a march without a marcher, verbal responses without a speaker, or a punch without a puncher? I hope that this statement does not prompt researchers to initiate studies in which plastic arms propelled by invisible strings strike objects in an effort to prove that people are dispensable sources of behavior.

Investigations of symbolic modeling (Bandura & Mischel, 1965; Bandura, Ross, & Ross, 1963a) demonstrate that matching performances can be readily achieved without requiring the physical presence of a model if the essential features of his behavior are accurately depicted either pictorially or verbally. To the extent that live and symbolic modeling convey the same amount of response information and are equally effective in commanding attention, they are likely to produce comparable levels of imitative behavior. Different forms of modeling, however, are not always equally efficacious. Performances that entail strong inhibitions may be more easily established through live demonstrations than by filmed presentations (Bandura & Menlove, 1968). One might also expect observers who lack conceptual skills to benefit less from verbal modeling than from behavioral demonstrations.

Establishment of new response patterns through the medium

of verbal modeling is often designated as "instructions" and distinguished from modeling as though they represented dissimilar influence procedures. In examining the process of verbal control of behavior it is essential to distinguish between the instigational and the modeling functions of instructions. Words can be used to impel people to perform previously learned activities and to teach them new behaviors. Instructions are most likely to produce correct performances when they both instigate a person to respond and describe the requisite behaviors and the manner in which they are to be executed. Little would be gained by simply ordering a person who had had no prior contact with cars to drive an automobile. In studies ostensibly comparing the relative efficacy of instructions and verbal modeling (Masters & Branch, 1970), both types of influences produce their effects through verbal modeling and they differ only in the explicitness with which the desired responses are defined. Greater performance gains are attained when desired behavior is clearly specified than when it must be inferred from a few examples.

Explanations of modeling phenomena usually cease at the point where modeling stimuli are attributed informative functions. As shown earlier, the psychological analysis must be extended beyond this level to explain how information conveyed by modeling stimuli is coded, the representational forms in which it is stored, and the process whereby representation guides action. Modeling stimuli assuredly do more than just convey information. They can also produce strong emotional and evaluative consequences that significantly affect both acquisition of new patterns of behavior and performance of existing ones (Bandura, 1971a).

The Role of Reinforcement in Observational Learning

An issue of considerable interest is whether reinforcement is necessary for imitative learning. As previously noted, reinforcement-oriented theorists (Baer & Sherman, 1964; Miller & Dollard, 1941; Gewirtz & Stingle, 1968) assume that imitative behavior must be reinforced in order to be learned. Social learning theory (Bandura, 1965b; 1969a) distinguishes between acquisition and performance of matching behavior. According to this view, imitative learning can occur through discriminative observation of modeled events and accompanying cognitive activities in the absence of external reinforcement. It is evident, however, that mere exposure to modeling stimuli is not in itself sufficient to produce imitative learning since not all stimulation impinging on individuals is necessarily observed by them. An adequate theory must include factors that exercise control over attending responses.

Anticipation of reinforcement is one of several variables that can influence what is observed and what goes unnoticed. Knowledge that performance of matching behavior produces valued rewards or averts punishment is likely to increase attentiveness to models whose behavior has functional value. Thus, reinforcement, through its incentive motivational effects, may indirectly affect the course of imitative learning by enhancing and focusing observing responses. Moreover, anticipated consequences can strengthen retention of what has been learned observationally by motivating people to code and to rehearse modeled responses that have utilitarian value. Controversy among theories of modeling centers on the manner in which reinforcement influences learning since all theorists agree that it does play a role in the acquisition process. As shown in the diagrammatic representation, the question in dispute is whether reinforcement functions retrospectively to strengthen preceding responses and their association to stimuli, or whether it facilitates learning through its effects on attentional, organizational, and rehearsal processes.

Reinforcement Theories

$$S_{\text{modeling}} \rightarrow R \rightarrow S^{\text{Reinf.}}$$
$$\text{stimuli}$$

Social Learning Theory

$$\text{Anticipated } S^{\text{Reinf.}} \rightarrow \text{Attention} \rightarrow S_{\text{modeling}} \rightarrow \begin{cases} \text{Symbolic Coding} \\ \text{Cognitive Organization} \\ \text{Rehearsal} \end{cases} \rightarrow R$$
$$\text{stimuli}$$

In social learning theory reinforcement is considered a facilitatory rather than a necessary condition because factors other than response consequences can also exercise selective control over attention. People will learn modeled events that command attention because of their striking physical properties, or because they have acquired distinctiveness and affective valence through prior experiences. One does not have to be reinforced to hear compelling auditory stimuli, to look at prominent visual displays, or to gaze at fetching belles. Indeed, when attention is effectively channeled to modeling stimuli through physical means, the addition of positive incentives does not affect the level of observational learning (Bandura, Grusec, & Menlove, 1966). Children who watched intently modeled activities presented on a television screen in a room darkened to eliminate distractions later displayed the same amount of imitative learning regardless of whether they were informed in advance that correct imitations would be rewarded or were given no prior incentives to learn the modeled performances. Anticipated positive consequences for matching behavior would be expected to influence self-regulated observational learning in which individuals can choose whom they will observe and for what length of time.

Both operant conditioning and social learning theories assume that performance of acquired matching behavior is strongly controlled by its consequences. But in social learning theory, behavior is regulated not only by directly experienced consequences arising from external sources, but also by vicarious reinforcement and self-reinforcement (Bandura, 1971a). In everyday life people continually observe the actions of others and the occasions on which they are rewarded, ignored, or punished. Observed consequences not only influence performance of similar behavior; they also determine whether a particular external reinforcer will function as a reward or as a punishment. Since direct and vicarious reinforcement occur together under natural conditions, the maintenance of behavior can best be understood by considering the interactive effects of these two sources of influence.

Not all human behavior is controlled by immediate external reinforcement. People regulate their own actions to some extent by self-generated anticipatory and self-evaluative consequences. At this higher level of psychological functioning, people set themselves certain performance standards, and they respond to their own behavior in self-rewarding or self-punishing ways, depending on whether their performances fall short of, match, or exceed their self-imposed demands. After a self-monitored reinforcement system is established, a given performance produces two sets of consequences—a self-evaluative reaction as well as some external outcome. In many instances self-produced and external consequences may conflict, as when externally approved courses of action, when carried out, give rise to self-devaluative reactions. Under these circumstances, the effects of self-reinforcement may prevail over external influences. Conversely, response patterns may be effectively maintained by self-reward under conditions of minimal external support or approval.

Interpretation of Vicarious Reinforcement

It is possible to arrange laboratory situations in which an individual observes another's behavior without seeing the consequences it produces. However, in everyday life modeled performances are invariably accompanied by outcomes which affect the degree to which observers act in a similar manner. The term vicarious reinforcement is applied to changes in the behavior of observers that result from witnessing a model's actions being rewarded or punished. As in the case of direct reinforcement, the influence of vicarious reinforcement varies according to the conditions under which it is administered, and whether the effects are measured in terms of learning or performance.

When individuals observe a single sequence of behavior followed by different outcomes they learn what they have seen regardless of whether the model's actions are rewarded, punished, or ignored (Bandura, 1965b). When a model is repeatedly reinforced as he displays an ongoing series of responses, observation of reinforcing consequences occurring early in the sequence might increase observers' attentiveness to the behavior that the model subsequently displays. People are inclined to pay little attention to models who have proved ineffectual but to observe closely models whose actions have been successful in the past. Vicarious reinforcement can indirectly affect the course of observational learning if repeated opportunities are given to observe modeled performances, the observer values the observed consequences, and he assumes that matching behavior will produce similar outcomes for him.

Imitative behavior is generally increased by observed reward and decreased by observed punishment. It should be noted here that vicarious reinforcement is simply a descriptive term that does not contain any explanation of how observed consequences affect behavior. Several different formulations have been proposed to explain its mode of operation.

According to Lewis and Duncan (1958), during the acquisition phase the model's responses elicit covert verbalizations in observers. The observed consequences are also experienced vicariously. As a result of contiguous occurrence, the pleasurable effects of observed reward and the frustrative effects of observed nonreward become conditioned to the observer's covert verbalizations. It is further assumed that these vicariously established emotions are transmitted from verbalizations to similar motor actions on the basis of prior associations between the two modes of responding.

There is some evidence that observers can develop conditioned emotional reactions as a result of seeing others endure painful consequences. It remains to be demonstrated whether observed nonreward is emotionally arousing to observers; whether observers covertly verbalize the model's instrumental responses while observing them performed; and whether emotional properties are, in fact, conditioned to verbalizations. In the more cognitive interpretation of classical conditioning (Bandura, 1969a), if a stimulus is paired with aversive experiences, the stimulus alone can produce emotional responses, not because it is invested with emotional properties, but because it tends to elicit emotion-arousing thoughts. In other words, the emotional responses are to a large extent cognitively induced rather than automatically evoked by the conditioned stimuli. From this perspective, performance of responses that individuals had previously seen punished can instigate anticipatory self-arousal without requiring that emotional responses be conditioned initially to covert verbalizations which serve as a vehicle for connecting emotions to overt actions.

Proponents of the operant conditioning view emphasize the discriminative rather than the emotional conditioning functions of observed reinforcement. Consequences administered to a model are treated as discriminative stimuli which indicate to observers that responses belonging to the same general class are likely to be reinforced in a similar manner (Gewirtz & Stingle, 1968). Since observed consequences are not present to serve as guiding stimuli when imitative behavior is performed, presumably the distinctive features of the environment or the behavior itself assume the controlling role.

According to social learning theory (Bandura, 1971a), vicarious reinforcement may operate through at least six different mechanisms to produce psychological changes in observers. One explanation is in terms of the *informative function* of observed outcomes. Response consequences experienced by other people convey information to observers about the type of behavior that is likely to meet with approval or disapproval. Knowledge about probable response consequences can aid in facilitating or inhibiting analogous responding. Unlike the operant conditioning interpretation, the social learning formulation assumes that imitative behavior is regulated by observers' judgments of probable consequences for prospective actions rather than being directly controlled by stimuli that were correlated with reinforcement. The influential role of cognitive regulatory factors is revealed in studies (Bandura & Barab, 1971) showing that erroneous judgments about likely response consequences may be more powerful in controlling imitative behavior, at least for a time, than discriminative stimuli and the actual effects the responses produce. These findings are consistent with research on nonimitative behavior (Kaufman, Baron, & Kopp, 1966) demonstrating that the reinforcement schedules people believe to be in effect can outweigh the influence of the reinforcements that are actually imposed on their behavior.

When the same behavior is treated differently depending on the social circumstances under which it is performed (as is often the case), vicarious reinforcement enables observers to identify situations in which the modeled activities are likely to be well received or censured. The resultant *environmental discriminations* (McDavid, 1964; Wilson, 1958) may facilitate performance of matching behavior in situations where the model previously responded with favorable consequences. Conversely, individuals will refrain from behaving imitatively in situations in which they have seen others punished for similar actions.

Observed reinforcement is not only informative but it can also have *incentive motivational effects.* Seeing others reinforced with valued incentives functions as a motivator by arousing the observer's expectations that he will be similarly rewarded for imitative behavior. Anticipation of rewards determines the speed, intensity, and persistence with which matching behavior is performed (Bruning, 1965; Rosenbaum & Bruning, 1966; Berger & Johansson, 1968).

Models generally exhibit emotional reactions while undergoing rewarding or punishing experiences. Observers are easily aroused by the emotional expressions of others. These vicariously elicited emotional responses can become conditioned either to the modeled behavior itself or to environmental stimuli that are regularly associated with performers' distress reactions (Bandura & Rosenthal, 1966; Berger, 1962; Craig & Weinstein, 1965). As a consequence, later performance of similar responses by the observer or the presence of negatively valenced stimuli is likely to evoke fear and response suppression. Emotional arousal and behavioral inhibitions can also be extinguished by having fearful observers watch performers engage in the threatening activity without experiencing any adverse consequences (Bandura, 1971b). *Vicarious conditioning and extinction of emotional arousal* may, therefore, partially account for the behavioral suppression or facilitation that results from observing affective consequences accruing to models.

In addition to the aforementioned effects of vicarious reinforcement, social status can be conferred on performers by the manner in which their behavior is reinforced. Punishment tends to devalue the model and his behavior, whereas the same model would be a source of emulation if his actions were praised and otherwise rewarded (Bandura, Ross, & Ross, 1963b; Hastorf, 1965). *Modification of model status* influences the degree to which observers pattern their own actions after behavior exemplified by different models.

Observed reinforcements can alter the *valuation of reinforcing agents* as well as recipients. When people misuse their power to reward and punish they undermine the legitimacy of their authority and generate strong resentment. Seeing inequitable punishment may free incensed observers from self-censure of their own actions, rather than prompting compliance, and thus increase transgressive behavior. Otherwise considerate people can readily be provoked to behave cruelly without remorse by observed injustice. Vicarious reinforcement, depending on its nature and context, may thus affect the level of imitative responding through any one or more of the processes discussed above.

Maintenance of Nonreinforced Modeling

Closely related to the issue of whether reinforcement is indispensable for observational learning are the explanations of why people continue to perform imitative responses that are not explicitly reinforced. Baer (Baer, Peterson, & Sherman, 1967; Baer & Sherman, 1964) and other researchers working within the operant conditioning framework (Lovaas, 1967), have interpreted the phenomenon, which they label "generalized imitation," in terms of conditioned reinforcement. The hypothesis assumes that repeated positive reinforcement of matching responses endows similarity with rewarding properties. After similarity has become reinforcing in itself persons are disposed to perform imitative responses for their inherent reward value.

Explanation of nonreinforced imitation in terms of conditioned reinforcement has been questioned by other investigators on both conceptual and empirical grounds (Bandura & Barab, 1971; Steinman, 1970a, b; Zahn & Yarrow, 1970). The theory explains more than has ever been observed. If behavioral similarity is inherently rewarding, then people should imitate all types of behaviors they see modeled, whereas, in fact, people tend to be highly selective in the behaviors they adopt from others (Bandura, 1969b). A conditioned reinforcement interpretation would have to posit counteracting influences to explain why people do not imitate indiscriminately everything they happen to observe.

A number of experiments have been performed to evaluate alternative hypotheses about the conditions governing nonreinforced imitation. The laboratory procedure that is commonly used to demonstrate the occurrence of nonreinforced imitation (Baer & Sherman, 1964) includes a variety of extraneous rewards and coercive pressures for imitative responding. One of the more forceful influences occurs when models instruct children to perform the demonstrated behavior and wait expectantly for aversively long intervals when children fail to respond imitatively. As might be expected, nonreinforced imitations assumed to be maintained by their inherent reward value cease when external social controls are removed (Peterson & Whitehurst, 1970; Steinman, 1970a, b; Zahn & Yarrow, 1970).

In everyday life imitative behavior is often performed without explicit external reinforcement even when coercive social controls are absent. This phenomenon may be partly attributable to discrimination processes. It has been demonstrated that people regulate their behavior to a large extent on the basis of anticipated consequences. These anticipated consequences are established on the basis of differential reinforcements that individuals have previously experienced in relation to different behavior, different people, and different situations; they are inferred from observed response consequences of others; or they may be conveyed through verbal explanations. In many instances, these various sources of information about reinforcement contingencies conflict. The problem of accurately assessing probable consequences is further complicated by the fact that diverse outcomes are often due to subtle differences in behavior. The same behavior may be rewarded, ignored, or punished depending upon the person toward whom it is expressed, the social setting in which it is exhibited, temporal considerations, and many other factors.

According to the discrimination hypothesis, nonrewarded imitations persist in the absence of extraneous social controls because individuals fail to discriminate the basis on which diverse modeled behaviors are reinforced. Support for this interpretation is provided in a study by Bandura and Barab (1971) that measured imitation as a function of differential consequences conveyed by model characteristics and features of the behavior itself. Children discontinued imitating nonrewarding models and nonreinforced responses that were easily distinguishable, but they continued to perform nonrewarded matching responses that were difficult to discriminate from rewarded imitations.

The overall research findings cast serious doubt on the view that response similarity functions as a conditioned reinforcer in maintaining imitative behavior. However, such behavior can be rendered partially independent of its external consequences through self-reinforcement of imitative performances. To the extent that individuals respond self-approvingly when they achieve close matches to meritorious performances, they can reinforce their own behavior without the necessity of external reinforcement.

Correlates of Modeling

In discussions of imitation the question often arises as to the types of people who are most responsive to modeling influences, and the kinds of models most likely to evoke imitative behavior from others. A great deal of research has been published on this topic (Bandura & Walters, 1963, Campbell, 1961; Flanders, 1968), but the generality of the findings is open to question because of the limited conditions under which observer and model correlates of imitative behavior have been measured.

It is often reported that persons who lack self-esteem, feel incompetent, are highly dependent, of low intelligence, or who have been frequently rewarded for imitative responses are especially prone to adopt the behavior of successful models. These prosaic correlates are based mainly on results from ambiguous experimental situations in which unfamiliar models perform inconsequential responses that have little or no functional value for subjects. In such situations the main rewards for brighter and bolder subjects are derived from outwitting the experimenter by disregarding the modeling influences.

Unfortunately, there is a paucity of research studying the degree to which people differing in intelligence, perceptiveness, and confidence emulate idealized models and those whose behavior has high utilitarian value. It is exceedingly unlikely that dull, dependent, and self-devaluative students would profit more from observing skillful performances by ski instructors, brain surgeons, airline pilots, or ingenious researchers than understudies who are bright, attentive and self-assured. When modeling influences are explicitly employed to teach people how to communicate effectively, how to conduct themselves in given interpersonal situations, and how to perform occupational activities competently, the more venturesome and talented are apt to derive the greater benefits from observation of exemplary models.

The traditional model correlates of imitation should also be accepted with reservation for similar reasons. It has been abundantly documented in social-psychological research (Bandura, 1969b; Blake, 1958; Campbell, 1961) that models who are high in prestige, power, intelligence, and competence are emulated to a considerably greater degree than models of subordinate standing. The influence of model status on matching behavior is generally explained in terms of differential reinforcement and generalization processes (Miller & Dollard, 1941). According to this interpretation, the behavior of high status models is more likely to be successful in achieving desired outcomes, and hence have greater value for observers, than the behavior of models who possess relatively low vocational, intellectual and social competencies. As a result of experiencing different outcomes for imitating models who possess diverse attributes, the identifying characteristics and status-conferring symbols assume informative value in signifying the probable consequences associated with behavior exemplified by different models. The effect of a model's prestige tends to generalize from one area of behavior to another and even to unfamiliar models who share characteristics with known reward-producers.

Model characteristics exert the greatest influence on imitation under conditions in which individuals can observe the model's behavior but not its consequences. When the value of modeled behavior is not revealed, observers must rely on such cues as clothing, linguistic style, general appearance, age, sex, likeableness, and various competence and status symbols as the basis for judging the probable efficacy of the modeled modes of response. Since the informative value of these cues is mainly derived from their correlation with reinforcement in the observer's past experience, they may not always be reliable predictors of how useful the behavior of new models, who happen to resemble former persons in some way, might be.

Ordinarily, modeled performances produce evident outcomes both for the model and the imitator. Response consequences generally outweigh model characteristics in promoting imitative behavior. One would not expect matching behavior that is primarily sustained by anticipatory consequences arising from model attributes to survive for long in the face of actual adverse outcomes. A prestigious or attractive model may induce a person to try a given course of action, but if the behavior should prove unsatisfactory, it will be discarded and the model's future influence diminished. For these reasons, studies conducted under conditions in which response consequences are not displayed may exaggerate the role played by model characteristics in the long-term control of imitative behavior.

REFERENCES

ADLER, L. L., & ADLER, H. E. 1968. Age as a factor in observational learning in puppies. *American Dachshund,* 13–14.

ALLPORT, F. H. 1924. *Social psychology.* Cambridge, Mass.: Riverside Press.

ARONFREED, J. 1969. The problem of imitation. In L. P. Lipsitt & H. W. Reese (Eds.), *Advances in child development and behavior.* Vol. IV. New York: Academic Press. Pp. 210–319.

BAER, D. M., Peterson, R. F., & Sherman, J. A. 1967. The development of imitation by reinforcing behavioral similarity to a model. *Journal of the Experimental Analysis of Behavior,* 10, 405–416.

BAER, D. M., & Sherman, J. A. 1964. Reinforcement control of generalized imitation in young children. *Journal of Experimental Child Psychology,* 1, 37–49.

BANDURA, A. 1960. Relationship of family patterns to child behavior disorders. Progress Report, Stanford University, Project No. M–1734, United States Public Health Service.

BANDURA, A. 1965a. Vicarious processes: A case of no-trial learning. In L. Berkowitz (Ed.), *Advances in experimental social psychology.* Vol. II. New York: Academic Press. Pp. 1–55.

BANDURA, A. 1956b. Behavioral modifications through modeling procedures. In L. Krasner & L. P. Ullmann (Eds.), *Research in behavior modification.* New York: Holt, Rinehart & Winston. Pp. 310–340.

BANDURA, A. 1969a. *Principles of behavior modification.* New York: Holt, Rinehart & Winston.

BANDURA, A. 1969b. Social-learning theory of identificatory processes. In D. A. Goslin (Ed.), *Handbook of socialization theory and research.* Chicago: Rand McNally. Pp. 213–262.

BANDURA, A. 1971a. Vicarious and self-reinforcement processes. In R. Glaser (Ed.), *The nature of reinforcement.* Columbus, Ohio: Merrill.

BANDURA, A. 1971b. Psychotherapy based upon modeling principles. In A. E. Bergin & S. L. Garfield (Eds.), *Handbook of psychotherapy and behavior change.* New York: Wiley. Pp. 653–708.

BANDURA, A. 1971c. *Social learning theory.* New York: General Learning Press.

BANDURA, A., & Barab, P. G. 1971. Conditions governing nonreinforced imitation. *Developmental Psychology,* 4 (in press)

BANDURA, A., Blanchard, E. B., & Ritter, B. 1969. The relative efficacy of desensitization and modeling approaches for inducing behavioral, affective, and attitudinal changes. *Journal of Personality and Social Psychology,* 13, 173–199.

BANDURA, A., GRUSEC, J. E., & MENLOVE, F. L. 1966. Observational learning as a function of symbolization and incentive set. *Child Development,* 37, 499–506.

BANDURA, A., GRUSEC, J. E., & MENLOVE, F. L. 1967a. Some social determinants of self-monitoring reinforcement systems. *Journal of Personality and Social Psychology,* 5, 449–455.

BANDURA, A., GRUSEC, J. E., & MENLOVE, F. L. 1967b. Vicarious extinction of avoidance behavior. *Journal of Personality and Social Psychology,* 5, 16–23.

BANDURA, A., & HARRIS, M. B. 1966. Modification of syntactic style. *Journal of Experimental Child Psychology,* 4, 341–352.

BANDURA, A., & HUSTON, A. C. 1961. Identification as a process of incidental learning. *Journal of Abnormal and Social Psychology,* 63, 311–318.

BANDURA, A., & JEFFERY, R. 1971. The role of symbolic coding, cognitive organization, and rehearsal in observational learning. Unpublished manuscript, Stanford University.

BANDURA, A., & McDONALD, F. J. 1963. The influence of social reinforcement and the behavior of models in shaping children's moral judgments. *Journal of Abnormal and Social Psychology,* 67, 274–281.

BANDURA, A., & MENLOVE, F. L. 1968. Factors determining vicarious extinction of avoidance behavior through symbolic modeling. *Journal of Personality and Social Psychology,* 8, 99–108.

BANDURA, A., & MISCHEL, W. 1965. Modification of self-imposed delay of reward through exposure to live and symbolic models. *Journal of Personality and Social Psychology,* 2, 698–705.

BANDURA, A., & ROSENTHAL, T. L. 1966. Vicarious classical conditioning as a function of arousal level. *Journal of Personality and Social Psychology,* 3, 54–62.

BANDURA, A., ROSS, D., & ROSS, S. A. 1963a. Imitation of film-mediated aggressive models. *Journal of Abnormal and Social Psychology,* 66, 3–11.

BANDURA, A., ROSS, D., & ROSS, S. A. 1963b. A comparative test of the status envy, social power, and secondary reinforcement theories of identificatory learning. *Journal of Abnormal and Social Psychology,* 67, 527–534.

BANDURA, A., & WALTERS, R. H. 1959. *Adolescent aggression.* New York: Ronald.

BANDURA, A., & WALTERS, R. H. 1963. *Social learning and personality development.* New York: Holt, Rinehart & Winston.

BENTON, A. A. 1967. Effect of the timing of negative response consequences on the observational learning of resistance to temptation in children. *Dissertation Abstracts,* 27, 2153–2154.

BERGER, S. M. 1962. Conditioning through vicarious instigation. *Psychological Review,* 69, 450–466.

BERGER, S. M., & JOHANSSON, S. L. 1968. Effect of a model's expressed emotions on an observer's resistance to extinction. *Journal of Personality and Social Psychology,* 10, 53–58.

BLACK, A. H. 1958. The extinction of avoidance responses under curare. *Journal of Comparative and Physiological Psychology,* 51, 519–524.

BLACK, A. H., CARLSON, N. J., & SOLOMON, R. L. 1962. Exploratory studies of the conditioning of autonomic responses in curarized dogs. *Psychological Monographs,* 76, No. 29 (Whole No. 548).

BLAKE, R. R. 1958. The other person in the situation. In R. Tagiuri & L. Petrullo (Eds.), *Person perception and interpersonal behavior.* Stanford, Calif.: Stanford University Press. Pp. 229–242.

BLANCHARD, E. B. 1970. The relative contributions of modeling, informational influences, and physical contact in the extinction of phobic behavior. *Journal of Abnormal Psychology,* 76, 55–61.

BROWN, R., & BELLUGI, U. 1964. Three processes in the child's acquisition of syntax. *Harvard Educational Review,* 34, 133–151.

BRUNING, J. L. 1965. Direct and vicarious effects of a shift in magnitude of reward on performance. *Journal of Personality and Social Psychology,* 2, 278–282.

CAMPBELL, D. T. 1961. Conformity in psychology's theories of acquired behavioral dispositions. In I. A. Berg & B. M. Bass (Eds.), *Conformity and deviation.* New York: Harper. Pp. 101–142.

CARROLL, W. R., ROSENTHAL. T. L., & BRYSH, C. G. 1969. The social transmission of grammatical parameters. Unpublished manuscript, University of Arizona.

COATES, B., & HARTUP, W. W. 1969. Age and verbalization in observational learning. *Developmental Psychology,* 1, 556–562.

COWAN, P. A., LANGER, J., HEAVENRICH, J., & NATHANSON, M. 1969. Social learning and Piaget's cognitive theory of moral development. *Journal of Personality and Social Psychology,* 11, 261–274.

CRAIG, K. D., & WEINSTEIN, M. S. 1965. Conditioning vicarious affective arousal. *Psychological Reports,* 17, 955–963.

CROOKS, J. L. 1967. Observational learning of fear in monkeys. Unpublished manuscript, University of Pennsylvania.

DUBANOSKI, R., & PARTON, D. 1968. Imitation without a model. Paper presented at the Eastern Psychological Association meeting, Washington, 1968.

EMMERICH, W. 1959. Parental identification in young children. *Genetic Psychology Monographs,* 60, 257–308.

ERVIN, S. M. 1964. Imitation and structural change in children's language. In E. H. Lenneberg (Ed.), *New directions in the study of language.* Cambridge, Mass.: M. I. T. Press. Pp. 163–189.

FLANDERS, J. P. 1968. A review of research on imitative behavior. *Psychological Bulletin,* 69, 316–337.

FOSS, B. M. 1964. Mimicry in mynas *(Gracula religiosa):* A test of Mowrer's theory. *British Journal of Psychology,* 55, 85–88.

FOUTS, G. T., & PARTON, D. A. 1969. Imitation: Effects of movement and static events. *Journal of Experimental Child Psychology,* 8, 118–126.

GERST, M. S. 1971. Symbolic coding processes in observational learning. *Journal of Personality and Social Psychology,* 19, 9–17.

GEWIRTZ, J. L., & STINGLE, K. G. 1968. Learning of generalized imitation as the basis for identification. *Psychological Review,* 75, 374–397.

GRUSEC, J. E. 1966. Some antecedents of self-criticism. *Journal of Personality and Social Psychology,* 4, 244–252.

GUTHRIE, E. R. 1952. *The psychology of learning.* New York: Harper.

HASTORF, A. H. 1965. The "reinforcement" of individual actions in a group situation. In L. Krasner & L. P. Ullmann (Eds.), *Research in behavior modification.* New York: Holt, Rinehart & Winston. Pp. 268–284.

HENKER, B. A. 1964. The effect of adult model relationships on children's play and task imitation. *Dissertation Abstracts,* 24, 4797.

HOLT, E. B. 1931. Animal drive and the learning process, Vol. 1. New York: Holt, Rinehart, and Winston.

HUMPHREY, G. 1921. Imitation and the conditioned reflex. *Pedadogical Seminary,* 28, 1–21.

JOHN, E. R., CHESLER, P., BARTLETT, F., & VICTOR, I. 1968. Observation learning in cats. *Science,* 159, 1489–1491.

KAUFMAN, A., BARON, A., & KOPP, R. E. 1966. Some effects of instructions on human operant behavior. *Psychonomic Monograph Supplements,* 1, 243–250.

KEENEY, T. J., CANNIZZO, S. R., & FLAVELL, J. H. 1967. Spontaneous and induced verbal rehearsal in a recall task. *Child Development,* 38, 953–966.

KELLER, H. 1927. *The story of my life.* New York: Doubleday Page.

KOHLBERG, L. 1963. Moral development and identification. In H. W. Stevenson (Ed.), *Child psychology: The sixty-second yearbook of the National Society for the Study of Education.* Part I. Chicago: National Society for the Study of Education. Pp. 277–332.

LAZOWICK, L. 1955. On the nature of identification. *Journal of Abnormal and Social Psychology,* 51, 175–183

LE FURGY, W. G., & WOLOSHIN, G. W. 1969. Immediate and long-term effects of experimentally induced social influences in the modification of adolescents' moral judgments. *Journal of Personality and Social Psychology,* 12, 104–110.

LENNEBERG, E. H. 1962. Understanding language without ability to speak. *Journal of Abnormal and Social Psychology,* 65, 419–425.

LEWIS, D. J., & DUNCAN, C. P. 1958. Vicarious experience and partial reinforcement. *Journal of Abnormal and Social Psychology,* 57, 321–326.

LIEBERT, R. M., ODOM, R. D., HILL, J. H., & HUFF, R. L. 1969. Effects of age and rule familiarity on the production of modeled language constructions. *Developmental Psychology,* 1, 108–112.

LOVAAS, O. I. 1967. A behavior therapy approach to the treatment of childhood schizophrenia. In J. P. Hill (Ed.), *Minnesota symposia on child psychology.* Vol. 1. Minneapolis: University of Minnesota Press. Pp. 108–159.

LOVAAS, O. I., REHM, R., & SCHREIBMAN, L. 1969. Attentional deficits in autistic children to multiple stimulus inputs. Unpublished manuscript, University of California, Los Angeles.

LUCHINS, A. S., & LUCHINS, E. H. 1966. Learning a complex ritualized social role. *Psychological Record,* 16, 177–187.

McDAVID, J. W. 1962. Effects of ambiguity of environmental cues upon learning to imitate. *Journal of Abnormal and Social Psychology,* 65, 381–386.

McDAVID, J. W. 1964. Effects of ambiguity of imitative cues upon learning by observation. *Journal of Social Psychology,* 62, 165–174.

McDougall, W. 1908. *An introduction to social psychology*. London: Methuen.

Masters, J. C., & Branch, M. N. 1969. Comparison of the relative effectiveness of instructions, modeling, and reinforcement procedures for inducing behavior change. *Journal of Experimental Psychology*, 80, 364–368.

Menyuk, P. 1964. Alteration of rules in children's grammar. *Journal of Verbal Learning and Verbal Behavior*, 3, 480–488.

Michael, D. N., & Maccoby, N. 1961. Factors influencing the effects of student participation on verbal learning from films: Motivating versus practice effects, "feedback," and overt versus covert responding. In A. A. Lumsdaine (Ed.) *Student response in programmed instruction*. Washington, D. C.: National Academy of Sciences—National Research Council, 1961. Pp. 271–293.

Miller, N. E. 1964. Some implications of modern behavior theory for personality change and psychotherapy. In P. Worchel & D. Byrne (Eds.), *Personality change*. New York: Wiley. Pp. 149–175.

Miller, N. E., & Dollard, J. 1941. *Social learning and imitation*. New Haven: Yale University Press.

Mischel, W., & Grusec, J. 1966. Determinants of the rehearsal and transmission of neutral and aversive behaviors. *Journal of Personality and Social Psychology*, 3, 197–205.

Morgan, C. L. 1896. *Habit and instinct*. London: Arnold.

Mowrer, O. H. 1950. Identification: A link between learning theory and psychotherapy. In *Learning theory and personality dynamics*. New York: Ronald. Pp. 573–615.

Mowrer, O. H. 1960. *Learning theory and behavior*. New York: Wiley.

Mussen, P. H., & Parker, A. L. 1965. Mother nurturance and girls' incidental imitative learning. *Journal of Personality and Social Psychology*, 2, 94–97.

Odom, R. D., Liebert, R. M., & Hill, J. H. 1968. The effects of modeling cues, reward, and attentional set on the production of grammatical and ungrammatical syntactic constructions. *Journal of Experimental Child Psychology*, 6, 131–140.

Parker, E. B. 1970. Information utilities and mass communication. In Harold Sackman & Norman Nie (Eds.), *Information Utility and Social Choice*, A.F.I.P.S. Press, Montvale, N. J. Pp. 51–70.

Parsons, T. 1951. *The social system*. New York: The Free Press of Glencoe.

Parsons, T. 1955. Family structure and the socialization of the child. In T. Parsons & R. F. Bales, *Family, socialization and interaction process*. Glencoe, Ill.: Free Press. Pp. 35–131.

Patterson, G. R., Littman, R. A., & Bricker, W. 1967. Assertive behavior in children: A step toward a theory of aggression. *Monographs of the Society for Research in Child Development*, 32, No. 5 (Serial No. 113).

Perloff, B. 1970. Influence of muscular relaxation and positive imagery on extinction of avoidance behavior through systematic desensitization. Unpublished doctoral dissertation, Stanford University.

Peterson, R. F., & Whitehurst, G. J. A variable influencing the performance of non-reinforced imitative behavior. *Journal of Applied Behavior Analysis*, 1970 (in press).

PIAGET, J. 1951. *Play, dreams, and imitation in childhood*. New York: Norton.

REICHARD, G. A. 1938. Social life. In F. Boas (Ed.), *General anthropology*. Boston: Health. Pp. 409–486.

ROSENBAUM, M. E., & BRUNING, J. L. 1966. Direct and vicarious effects of variations in percentage of reinforcement on performance. *Child Development*, 37, 959–966.

ROSENTHAL, T. L., & WHITEBOOK, J. S. 1970. Incentives versus instructions in transmitting grammatical parameters with experimenter as model. *Behaviour Research and Therapy*, 8, 189–196.

ROSENTHAL, T. L., & ZIMMERMAN, B. J. 1970. Modeling by exemplification and instruction in training conservation. Unpublished manuscript, University of Arizona.

ROSENTHAL, T. L., ZIMMERMAN, B. J., & DURNING, K. 1970. Observationally induced changes in children's interrogative classes. *Journal of Personality and Social Psychology*, 16, 681–688.

SHEFFIELD, F. D. 1961. Theoretical considerations in the learning of complex sequential tasks from demonstration and practice. In A. A. Lumsdaine (Ed.), *Student response in programmed instruction*. Washington, D. C.: National Academy of Sciences—National Research Council, 1961. Pp. 13–32.

SHEFFIELD, F. D., & MACCOBY, N. 1961. Summary and interpretation of research on organizational principles in constructing filmed demonstrations. In A. A. Lumsdaine (Ed.), *Student response in programmed instruction*. Washington, D. C.: National Academy of Sciences—National Research Council, 1961. Pp. 117–131.

SKINNER, B. F. 1953. *Science and human behavior*. New York: Macmillan.

SLOBIN, D. I. 1968. Imitation and grammatical development in children. In N. S. Endler, L. R. Boulter, & H. Osser (Eds.), *Contemporary issues in developmental psychology*. New York: Holt, Rinehart & Winston. Pp. 437–443.

SOLOMON, R. L., & TURNER, L. H. 1962. Discriminative classical conditioning in dogs paralyzed by curare can later control discriminative avoidance responses in the normal state. *Psychological Review*, 69, 202–219.

STEINMAN, W. M. 1970a. Generalized imitation and the discrimination hypothesis. *Journal of Experimental Child Psychology*, 10, 79–99.

STEINMAN, W. M. 1970b. The social control of generalized imitation. *Journal of Applied Behavior Analysis*, 3, 159–167.

STOKE, S. M. 1950. An inquiry into the concept of identification. *Journal of Genetic Psychology*, 76, 163–189.

STUMPHAUZER, J. S. 1969. Increased delay of gratification in young prison inmates through imitation of high-delay peer-models. Unpublished doctoral dissertation, Florida State University.

SULLIVAN, E. V. 1967. The acquisition of conservation of substance through film-mediated models. In D. W. Brison & E. V. Sullivan (Eds.), *Recent research on the acquisition of conservation of substance. Education Monograph*. Toronto: Ontario Institute for Studies in Education.

TARDE, G. 1903. *The laws of imitation*. New York: Holt, Rinehart, & Winston.

TAUB, E., BACON, R. C., & BERMAN, A. J. 1965. Acquisition of a trace-conditioned avoidance response after deafferentation of the responding limb. *Journal of Comparative and Physiological Psychology*, 59, 275–279.

TAUB, E., TEODORU, D., ELLMAN, S. J., BLOOM, R. F., & BERMAN, A. J. 1966. Deafferentation in monkeys: Extinction of avoidance responses, discrimination and discrimination reversal. *Psychonomic Science*, 4, 323–324.

THORNDIKE, E. L. 1898. Animal intelligence: An experimental study of the associative processes in animals. *Psychological Review Monograph Supplements*, 2, No. 4 (Whole No. 8).

VAN HEKKEN, S. M. J. 1969. The influence of verbalization on observational learning in a group of mediating and a group of non-mediating children. *Human Development*, 12, 204–213.

WALTERS, R. H., & PARKE, R. D. 1964. Influence of response consequences to a social model on resistance to deviation. *Journal of Experimental Child Psychology*, 1, 269–280.

WALTERS, R. H., PARKE, R. D., & CANE, V. A. 1965. Timing of punishment and the observation of consequences to others as determinants of response inhibition. *Journal of Experimental Child Psychology*, 2, 10–30.

WASSERMAN, L. Discrimination learning and development of learning sets in autistic children. Unpublished doctoral dissertation, University of California, Los Angeles, 1968.

WATSON, J. B. 1908. Imitation in monkeys. *Psychological Bulletin*, 5, 169–178.

WHEELER, L. 1966. Toward a theory of behavioral contagion. *Psychological Review*, 73, 179–192.

WILSON, W. C. 1958. Imitation and learning of incidental cues by preschool children. *Child Development*, 29, 393–397.

YOUNG, E. H., & HAWK, S. S. 1955. *Moto-kinesthetic speech training.* Stanford, Calif.: Stanford University Press.

ZAHN, C. J., & YARROW, M. R. 1970. Factors influencing imitative learning in preschool children. *Journal of Experimental Child Psychology*, 9, 115–130.

1

Mimicry in Mynas (Gracula Religiosa): A Test of Mowrer's Theory

BRIAN M. FOSS

Mowrer (1950, chap. 24) states that sounds must be associated with reinforcement for talking birds to imitate them. In his most recent formulation (Mowrer, 1960) the reasoning is as follows: if any stimulus, for instance the sight of a human being, is repeatedly associated with a primary reinforcer (e.g., food) then the appearance of the human will give rise to "hope," which in turn is reinforcing; if the human repeatedly utters a given sound, that sound will also produce hope; if now the bird, in the course of its babbling, makes noises which approximate those produced by the human, these will produce hope, and the production of the noises will be reinforced—the more so the more the noises approach the human version.

Reprinted by permission of The British Psychological Society from the BRITISH JOURNAL OF PSYCHOLOGY, 1964, Vol. 55, pp. 85–88.

Skinner (1957, p. 64) appears to accept this view, although he is not primarily concerned with factors affecting the first appearance of any response. He is concerned with the control of the response once it has appeared, and this has been shown to be possible with the utterances of mynas (Grosslight, Harrison, & Weiser, 1962).

Mowrer believes that imitation learning by talking birds can be taken as a model for other kinds of imitation. A child will tend to imitate noises of adults, especially those with whom he is identified, since they will have the greater reinforcing power. Obviously the exact mechanism of learning will be more complicated in cases other than learning to produce sounds. For sounds, the child can match his own utterances against those produced by the person being imitated, but it is not clear how this matching can happen when for example a movement is being imitated.

Some doubt is felt about Mowrer's theory for two reasons: (i) talking birds often pick up noises which are not consistently associated with reinforcement (e.g., the noise of a dripping tap); (ii) bird fanciers often recommend training birds to talk with the cage covered, and also by means of gramophone records (see, for example, *Pet Myna,* 1957), situations which seem to minimize the chances of hope, in Mowrer's sense.

The present experiment attempts a rough test of the theory that learning to utter a sound depends on the sound's being associated with reinforcement.

METHOD

Subjects

The subjects were two groups of Indian Hill Mynas *(Gracula Religiosa Intermedia)* bought as "gapers" and aged about 8 months at the start of the experiment. Group A consisted of two birds and group B of four. This difference in numbers was incidental to the experiment. Since these birds learn from each other, in a sense the experiment was done on two subjects. The two groups were treated slightly differently: group A were kept in a cage in the experimenter's room; group B were all in one cage in a room adjoining another which could be reached by the experimenter without the birds seeing or hearing him.

Procedure

The stimuli used were an ascending whistle *(X)*, going from 500 c.p.s. to 2000 c.p.s., in the space of 2 sec., and the same whistle reversed, and therefore descending *(Y)*. Each whistle was recorded on a loop of tape which repeated the whistle every 6½ seconds. This kind of whistle is not heard in the repertoire of an unsophisticated bird and its timbre was also unusual. This choice was made to help in identifying the whistles when the brids finally produced them, and also to minimize transfer. A whistling ban was imposed in the neighborhood of the cages.

The birds were trained as shown in Table 1.1.

TABLE 1.1: *Training Schedule*

| | Whistles | |
Birds	X	Y
Group A	Without reinforcement	With reinforcement
Group B	With reinforcement	Without reinforcement

This design did not allow for controlling which whistle was heard first for each group. To give Mowrer's theory priority, each group heard first the whistle associated with reinforcement, the number of repetitions of each whistle being gradually increased from 10 to 30 per session. The whistles associated with reinforcement were always played at midday, the others at dusk (Table 1.2).

At the midday sessions food was prepared in full view of the birds, and put in the cages (always by the same experimenter)

TABLE 1.2: *Numbers of Repetitions of Stimuli per Session*

	Midday (reinforcement)	Dusk (no reinforcement)
Day 1	10	10
Day 2	20	20
Day 3 onwards	30	30

while the appropriate whistle was being played. At the dusk sessions the groups were treated differently. Group A lives in a room where they saw many people and heard a good deal of conversation. Their cage was covered at least 15 minutes before the tape was played and remained covered for at least 30 minutes afterwards. During this period they heard no human vocal noises. For group B, living in an isolated room, the tape was switched on in an adjoining room, so that the birds neither heard nor saw a human during the session.

Recording Results

After 5 weeks (less 2 weekends) of this daily procedure, the procedure was stopped and recordings were made of each group, with and without the experimenter in the room. For group A a total of 12 hr. was sampled, for group B 9 hr., both spread over 3 days. The recordings were made at various times between 9:30 a.m. and dusk.

RESULTS

The birds tended to incorporate the test whistles into other whistling and babbling, and later (after the experiment was over) tended to construct variations on the original themes. However it was possible to count those whistles which were produced in isolation from other utterances, and which clearly had the correct timbre and the correct ascending or descending character. (The birds were successful in reproducing the whistles over only about half of the range of the test stimuli.) The results are shown in Table 1.3.

TABLE 1.3: *Numbers of Whistles Reproduced over the Times Sampled*

	Whistle associated with reinforcement	Whistle not associated with reinforcement
Group A	26	21
Group B	11	13

It is clear that both groups had learned both whistles. There was no tendency for one whistle rather than the other to be produced at any particular time of day. Group A produced whistles equally often while the experimenter was in and out of the room; group B never produced the whistles while the experimenter was near during the period under consideration. They did so for the first time several days after the experiment was finished.

Other Findings

It was not until recordings were made in group B's room in the absence of humans that it was discovered that these birds had acquired a repertoire of words, as well as the intended whistles. The tendency for mimicked noises to be produced at first when humans are not present had been observed with a previous collection of birds, and has also been reported by Thorpe (1961, p. 119). Recording of group A was not begun early enough to discover if they behaved similarly.

Both groups produced a great amount of babbling (group B almost entirely when no humans were present) which contained the phonemes of human speech but no words. From a distance it was indistinguishable from human conversation. This behavior is reminiscent of human prelingual babbling which is said to become restricted gradually to the phonemes of the adult language (Brown, 1958, pp. 199–200).

Babbling, and also native noises (shrieks and "grackle" noises), were set going by various stimuli—human conversation, the telephone ringing, doors banging. After the end of the experiment (this applies particularly to group B), if the test whistles were played, the birds frequently joined in, on occasion joining the whistle half way through its course and finishing it. This was done exactly on pitch, as far as can be detected.

DISCUSSION

The experiment showed that reinforcement did not play a part in determining which sounds the mynas would imitate. It might be argued that during the "reinforced" sessions the birds were distracted by the sight and anticipation of food, whereas in the "nonreinforced" sessions distractions were minimal. If this is so, it remains to be explained under what conditions a reinforcer is distracting rather than reinforcing; also it is difficult to see that any reinforcement at all could have been associated with the dusk sessions.

Since the birds in one group did their whistling (and almost all their babbling) when humans were not present, it may be that, once the response has been acquired, it has self-reinforcing properties. If so, these properties were not acquired (in the case of one of the whistles) through association with primary reinforcement. The fact that the birds came to "join in" with the test whistles suggests a kind of behavioral contagion rather than behavior for reinforcement's sake.

The result of this experiment is disappointing. Mowrer's theory was welcome in that it showed that this particular kind of imitation learning could be explained in terms of accepted principles of learning. One is left with the unsatisfactory alternative of saying that myna birds have a tendency to mimic.

REFERENCES

BROWN, R. 1958. *Words and Things*. Glencoe, Ill.: Free Press.
GROSSLIGHT, J. H., HARRISON, P. C., & WEISER, C. M. 1962. Reinforcement control of vocal responses in the myna bird *(Gracula Religiosa)*. *Psychological Record* 12, 193–201.

MOWRER, O. H. 1950. *Learning Theory and Personality Dynamics.* New York: Ronald Press.

MOWRER, O. H. 1960. *Learning Theory and the Symbolic Process.* New York: Wiley.

Pet Myna 1957. Fond du Lac, Wisc.: All-Pets Books Inc.

SKINNER, B. F. 1957. *Verbal Behaviour.* London: Methuen.

THORPE, W. H. 1961. *Bird-Song. Cambridge Monographs in Experimental Biology,* no. 12. Cambridge University Press.

2

A Comparative Test of The Status Envy, Social Power, and Secondary Reinforcement Theories of Identificatory Learning

ALBERT BANDURA
DOROTHEA ROSS
SHEILA A. ROSS

Although it is generally assumed that social behavior is learned and modified through direct reward and punishment of instrumental responses, informal observation and laboratory study of the social learning process reveal that new responses may be rapidly acquired and existing behavioral repertoires may be considerably changed as a function of observing the behavior and attitudes exhibited by models (Bandura, 1962).

The latter type of learning is generally labeled "imitation" in

Reprinted by permission of the publisher from the JOURNAL OF ABNORMAL AND SOCIAL PSYCHOLOGY, 1963, Vol. 67, pp. 527–534. Copyright 1963, American Psychological Association.

* This investigation was supported by Research Grant M-5162 from the National Institutes of Health, United States Public Health Service.

behavior theory, and "identification" in most theories of personality. These concepts, however, are treated in the present paper as synonymous since both encompass the same behavioral phenomenon, i.e., the tendency for a person to match the behavior, attitudes, or emotional reactions as exhibited by actual or symbolized models. While the defining properties of identification are essentially the same in different personality theories, a host of divergent learning conditions have been proposed as the necessary antecedent variables for matching or identificatory behavior (Bronfenbrenner, 1960; Freud, 1946; Freud, 1924, 1948; Kagan, 1958; Klein, 1949; Maccoby, 1959; Mowrer, 1950; Parsons, 1955; Sears, 1957; Whiting, 1960).

In the experiment reported in this paper predictions were derived from three of the more prominent theories of learning by identification, and tested in three-person groups representing prototypes of the nuclear family. In one condition of the experiment an adult assumed the role of controller of resources and positive reinforcers. Another adult was the consumer or recipient of these resources, while the child, a participant observer in the triad, was essentially ignored. In a second treatment condition, one adult controlled the resources; the child, however, was the recipient of the positive reinforcers and the other adult was assigned a subordinate and powerless role. An adult male and female served as models in each of the triads. For half the boys and girls in each condition the male model controlled and dispensed the rewarding resources, simulating the husband dominant family; for the remaining children, the female model mediated the positive resources as in the wife dominant home. Following the experimental social interactions the two adult models exhibited divergent patterns of behavior in the presence of the child, and a measure was obtained of the degree to which the child subsequently patterned his behavior after that of the models.

The authors are indebted to Beverly Busching, Malka Yaari, Nancy Wiggins, and John Steinbruner, who assisted in collecting the data.

This research was carried out while the junior author was the recipient of an American Association of University Women International Fellowship for postdoctoral research.

According to the *status envy theory* of identification recently proposed by Whiting (1959, 1960), where a child competes unsuccessfully with an adult for affection, attention, food, and care, the child will envy the consumer adult and consequently identify with him. Whiting's theory represents an extension of the Freudian defensive identification hypothesis that identificatory behavior is the outcome of rivalrous interaction between the child and the parent who occupies an envied consumer status. While Freud presents the child as in competition with the father primarily for the mother's sexual and affectional attention, Whiting regards any forms of reward, material and social, as valued resources around which rivalry may develop. The status envy theory thus predicts that the highest degree of imitation by the child will occur in the experimental condition in which the rivalrous adult consumes the resources desired by the child, with the consumer adult serving as the primary object of imitation.

In contrast to the envy theory, other writers (Maccoby, 1959; Mussen & Distler, 1959; Parsons, 1955) assume that the controller, rather than the consumer, of resources is the main source of imitative behavior. The *power theory* of social influence has received considerable attention in experimental social psychology, though not generally in the context of identification theories.

Social power is typically defined as the ability of a person to influence the behavior of others by controlling or mediating their positive and negative reinforcements. French and Raven (1959) have distinguished five types of power based on expertness, attractiveness, legitimacy, coerciveness, and rewarding power, each of which is believed to have somewhat differential effects on the social influence process. For example, the use of threat or coercion, in which the controller derives power from his ability to administer punishments, not only develops avoidance behavior toward the controller but also decreases his attractiveness and hence his effectiveness in altering the behavior of others beyond the immediate social influence setting (French, Morrison, & Levinger, 1960; Zipf, 1960). The use of reward power, in contrast, both fosters approach responses toward the power figure and increases his attractiveness or secondary reward value through the repeated association of his attributes with positive reinforcement. Attractiveness is assumed to extend the controller's power over a wide range in behavior (French & Raven, 1959).

In the present investigation power based upon the ability to dispense rewards was manipulated experimentally. In accordance with the social power theory of identification, but contrasting with the status envy hypothesis, one would predict that children will reproduce more of the behavior of the adult who controls positive reinforcers, than that of the powerless adult model, and that power inversions on the part of the male and female models will produce cross-sex imitation.

The *secondary reinforcement theory* of identification, which has been alluded to in the discussion of social power through attractiveness, has been elaborated in greatest detail by Mowrer (1950, 1958). According to this view, as a model mediates the child's biological and social rewards, the behavioral attributes of the model are paired repeatedly with positive reinforcement and thus acquire secondary reward value. On the basis of stimulus generalization, responses which match those of the model attain reinforcing value for the child in proportion to their similarity to those made by the model. Consequently, the child can administer positively conditioned reinforcers to himself simply by reproducing as closely as possible the model's positively valenced behavior. This theory predicts that the experimental condition in which the child was the recipient of positive reinforcements will yield the highest imitation scores with the model who dispensed the rewards serving as the primary source of imitative behavior.

METHOD

Subjects

The subjects were 36 boys and 36 girls enrolled in the Stanford University Nursery School. They ranged in age from 33 to

65 months, although the variability was relatively small with most of the ages falling around the mean of 51 months.

An adult male and female served as models in the triads so as to reproduce possible power structures encountered in different types of family constellations. A female experimenter conducted the study for all 72 children.

Design and Procedure

The subjects were assigned randomly to two experimental groups and one control group of 24 subjects each. Half the subjects in each group were males, and half were females.

High rewarding power was induced experimentally through the manipulation of material and social reinforcements, and the use of verbal structuring techniques. While accompanying the child to the experimental room, for example, the experimenter informed the child that the adult who assumed the role of controller owned the nursery school "surprise room," as well as a fabulous collection of play materials. After introducing the child to the controller, the experimenter asked whether the child might play in the surprise room. The controller explained that he was on his way to his car to fetch some of his most attractive toys, but the experimenter and the child could proceed to the room where he would join them shortly. As the controller left, the experimenter commented on how lucky they were to have access to the controller's play materials.

On the way to the experimental room they met the other adult who insisted on joining them but the experimenter informed her that she would have to obtain permission from the controller since he owned the room, and it was doubtful whether sufficient play materials were available for both the adult and the child. This brief encounter with the other adult was designed primarily to create the set that rewards were available to one person only and thereby to induce rivalrous feelings over the controller's resources.

As soon as the experimenter and the child arrived in the experimental room, they sat down at a small table and played with the few Lincoln Logs and two small cars that were provided. A short time later the other adult appeared and announced that the controller also granted her permission to play in the room.

The controller then entered carrying two large toy boxes containing a variety of highly attractive masculine and feminine toys, a colorful juice dispensing fountain, and an ample supply of cookies. As soon as the controller appeared on the scene, the experimenter departed.

For children in the Adult Consumer condition, the adult who assumed the role of consumer requested permission to play with the articles and the controller replied that, since the child appeared to be occupied at his table, the consumer was free to use the play materials. This monopolistic move by the consumer adult left the child stranded at a table with two relatively uninteresting toys.

During the 20-minute play session, the controller offered the consumer, among other things, miniature pinball machines, mechanical sparkling toys, kaleidoscopes, dolls, and actively participated with the consumer in dart games and other activities. To add to the credibility of the situation, both the controller and consumer devoted most of their attention to articles, such as the pinball machine and dart game, which could be used in adult appropriate activities. Throughout the interaction the controller was most helpful, supportive, and generous in dispensing social reinforcers in the form of praise, approval, and positive attention. The consumer, in turn, commented frequently on the controller's highly attractive resources so as to further enhance the controller's rewarding status. The consumer also verbalized considerable positive affect characteristic of a person experiencing positive reinforcements.

Approximately half way through the session, the controller remarked, "Say, you look hungry. I have just the thing for you." He then brought forth the soda fountain dispenser, poured colorful fruit juices into paper cups and served them to the consumer along with a generous supply of cookies. While the consumer was enjoying his snack, the controller turned on a "TV-radio" that played a nursery melody while a revolving dial displayed a series of storybook scenes.

Toward the end of the session, the controller informed the consumer that he would be leaving on a shopping trip to San Francisco that afternoon, and asked the consumer if there was anything special she would like him to buy for her. The consumer requested a super two-wheel bicycle, a high status object among the nursery school children. The controller promised to purchase the bicycle along with any other items the consumer might think of before the controller departed for the city.

The procedure for the Child Consumer condition was identical with that described above except the child was the recipient of the material rewards and the social reinforcement. During the session the other adult sat at the opposite end of the room engrossed in a book, and was totally ignored by the controller. In discussing the prospective San Francisco shopping trip, the controller mentioned to the child that he was planning to visit some toy stores in the city that afternoon, and asked for suggestions of attractive toys he might purchase for future play sessions with children.

For half the boys and girls in each treatment condition the male model controlled and dispensed the resources, simulating the husband dominant family; for the remaining children the female model mediated the positive resources as in the wife dominant home.

At the completion of the social interaction session the controller announced that he had a surprise game in his car that the three of them could play together. The controller then asked the other adult to fetch the experimenter to assist them with the game, and as soon as the adult departed, the controller removed the toys and assembled the imitation task apparatus.

Imitation Task

The imitation task was essentially the same two-choice discrimination problem utilized in an earlier experiment (Bandura & Huston, 1961), except the response repertoires exhibited by the models were considerably extended, and the procedure used in the acquisition trials was somewhat modified.

The apparatus consisted of two small boxes with hinged lids, identical in color and size. The boxes were placed on stools approximately 4 feet apart and 8 feet from the starting point. On the lid of each box was a rubber doll.

As soon as the other adult returned with the experimenter, the controller asked both the child and the experimenter to be seated in the chairs along the side of the room, and the other adult to stand at the starting point, while the controller described the game they were about to play. The controller then explained that the experimenter would hide a picture sticker in one of the two boxes and the object of the game was to guess which box contained the sticker. The adults would have the first set of turns, following which the child would play the guessing game.

The discrimination problem was employed simply as a cover task that occupied the children's attention while at the same time permitted observation of the models as they performed divergent patterns of behavior during the discrimination trials in the absence of any set to attend to or learn the responses exhibited by the models.

Before commencing the trials, the controller invited the other participants to join him in selecting a "thinking cap" from hat racks containing two identical sets of four sailor caps, each of which had a different colored feather. The controller selected the green feathered hat, remarked, "Feather in the front" and wore the hat with the feather facing forward. The other model selected the yellow feathered hat, commented, "Feather in the back," and placed the hat on her head with the feather facing backward. The child then made his choice from the four hats in the lower rack and it was noted whether he matched the color preference, hat placement, and the verbal responses of the one or the other model.

The models then went to the starting point, the child returned to his seat, and the experimenter loaded both boxes with sticker pictures for the models' trials.

During the execution of each trial, each model exhibited a different set of relatively novel verbal and motor responses that were totally irrelevant to the discrimination problem to which the child's attention was directed. At the starting point the controller stood with his arms crossed, but at the experimenter's warning not to look, the controller placed his hands over his eyes, faced sideways, and asked, "Ready?" The other model stood with his arms on his hips, then squatted with his back turned to the boxes, and asked, "Now?"

As soon as the experimenter gave the signal for the first trial, the controller remarked, "Forward march" and began marching slowly toward the designated box repeating, "March, march, march." When he reached the box he said, "Sock him," hit the doll aggressively off the box, opened the lid and yelled, "Bingo," as he reached down for the sticker. He then remarked, "Lickit-sticket," as he pressed on the picture sticker with his thumb in the upper-right quadrant of a 24 x 24 inch sheet of plain white paper that hung on the wall immediately behind the boxes. The controller terminated the trial by replacing the doll facing sideways on the container with the comment, "Look in the mirror," and made a final verbal response, "There."

The other model then took her turn and performed a different set of imitative acts but equated with the controller's responses in terms of number, types of response classes represented, structural properties, and interest value. At the starting point, for example, she remarked, "Get set, go" and walked stiffly toward the boxes repeating "Left, right, left, right." When she reached the container she said, "Down and up," as she lay the doll down on the lid and opened the box. She then exclaimed, "A stickeroo," repeated, "Weto-smacko," and slapped on the sticker with the open hand in the lower-left quadrant of the sheet of paper. In terminating the trial, the model lay the doll on the lid of the container with the remark, "Lie down," and returned with her hands behind her back, and emitted the closing remark, "That's it."

The two sets of responses were counterbalanced by having the models display each pattern with half the subjects in each of the three groups.

The models performed alternately for four trials. At the conclusion of the fourth trial the controller explained that he had to check some materials in his car and while he and the other model were away the child might take his turns. Before they departed, however, the experimenter administered a picture preference test in which the models were asked to select their preferred picture from six different stickers pasted on a 5 x 8 inch card, after which the child was presented a similar card containing an identical set of stickers and requested to indicate his preference.

In addition to the introductory block of four trials by the models, the child's 15 total test trials were interspersed with three two-trial blocks by the models. The models were always absent from the room during the child's test series. This procedure was adopted in order to remove any imagined situational restraints against, or coercion for, the child to reproduce the models' responses. Moreover, demonstrations of delayed imitation in the absence of the model provide more decisive evidence for learning by means of imitation.

The models always selected different boxes, the right-left position varying from trial to trial in a fixed irregular order, and the controller always took the first turn. Although the models received stickers on each trial, the child was nonrewarded on one third of the trials in order to maintain his interest in the cover task.

At the beginning of each of the blocks of subjects' trials, the experimenter administered the picture preference test and the selection of stickers that matched the models' choices was recorded. In addition, on the eighth trial the models removed their hats and hung them in different locations in the room. If the child removed his hat during the session and placed it along side one or the other of the model's hats, this imitative act was also scored.

At the completion of the imitation phase of the experiment, the children were interviewed by the experimenter in order to determine whom they considered to be the controller of resources, and to assess their model preferences. The latter data were used as an index of attraction to the models. In addition, for the children in the adult consumer condition, the session was concluded by providing them the same lavish treatment accorded their adult rival.

Children in the control group had no prior social interaction with the models but participated with them in the imitative learning phase of the study. The experimenter assumed complete charge of the procedures and treated the models as though they were naive subjects. This control group was included primarily to determine the models' relative effectiveness as modeling stimuli. In addition, the models alternated between subjects in the order in which they executed the trials so as to test for the possibility of a primacy or a recency of exposure effect on imitative behavior.

Imitation Scores

The imitation scores were obtained by summing the frequency of occurrence of the postural, verbal, and motor responses described in the preceding section, and the hat, color, and picture preferences that matched the selections of each of the two models.

The children's performances were scored by three raters who observed the experimental sessions through a one-way mirror from an adjoining observation room. The raters were provided with a separate check list of responses exhibited by each of the two models, and the scoring procedure simply involved checking the imitative responses performed by the children on each trial. In order to provide an estimate of interscorer reliability, the performances of 30% of the children were recorded simultaneously but independently by two observers. The raters were in perfect agreement on 95% of the specific imitative responses that they scored.

RESULTS

The control group data revealed that the two models were equally effective in eliciting imitative responses, the mean values being 17.83 and 20.46 for the male and female model, respectively; nor did the children display differential imitation of same-sex ($M = 20.30$) and opposite-sex ($M = 17.92$) models. Although children in the control group tended to imitate the second model ($M = 22.21$) to a somewhat greater extent than the one who performed first ($M = 16.08$) on each trial, suggesting a

TABLE 2.1: *Mean Number of Imitative Responses Performed by Subgroups of Children in the Experimental Triads*

Subjects	Objects of imitation			
	Male	Female	Female	Male
	Controller	Consumer	Controller	Consumer
Girls	29.00	9.67	26.00	10.00
Boys	30.17	18.67	22.33	16.17
Total	29.59	14.17	24.17	13.09
	Controller	Ignored	Controller	Ignored
Girls	22.00	16.17	31.84	22.17
Boys	29.17	16.67	26.83	34.50
Total	25.59	16.42	29.34	28.34

The assistance of Eleanor Willemsen with the statistical computations is gratefully acknowledged.

recency of exposure effect, the difference was not of statistically significant magnitude ($t = 1.60$).

Table 2.1 presents the mean imitation scores for children in each of the two experimental triads. A $2 \times 2 \times 2 \times 2$ mixed factorial analysis of variance was computed on these data in which the four factors in the design were sex of child, sex of the model who controlled the resources, adult versus child consumer, and the controller versus the other model as the source of imitative behavior. As shown in Table 2.2, the findings of this study clearly support the social power theory of imitation. In both experimental treatments, regardless of whether the rival adult or the children themselves were the recipients of the rewarding resources, the model who possessed rewarding power was imitated to a greater degree than was the rival or the ignored model ($F = 40.61$, $p < .001$). Nor did the condition combining resource ownership with direct reinforcement of the child yield the highest imitation of the model who controlled and dispensed the positive rewards. The latter finding is particularly surprising since an earlier experiment based on two-person groups (Bandura & Huston, 1961), demonstrated that pairing of model with positive reinforcement substantially enhanced the occurrence of imitative behavior. An examination of the remaining significant interaction effects together with the postexperimental interview data suggest a possible explanation for the discrepant results.

The differential in the controller-other model imitation was most pronounced when the male model was the controller of resources ($F = 4.76$, $p < .05$), particularly for boys. In fact, boys who were the recipients of rewarding resources mediated by the female model tended to favor the ignored male as their object of imitation. In the postexperiment interview a number of boys in this condition spontaneously expressed sympathy for the ignored male and mild criticism of the controller for not being more charitable with her bountiful resources (for example, "She doesn't share much. John played bravely even though she didn't even share. . . . She's a bit greedy.").

As a partial check on whether this factor would tend to diminish the differential imitation of the two models, six children—three boys and three girls—participated in a modified Child Consumer treatment in which, halfway through the social inter-action session, the ignored adult was informed that he too might have access to the playthings. He replied that he was quite content to read his book. This modified procedure, which removed the rivalry and the exclusion of the model, yielded four times as much imitation of the controller relative to the model who was ignored by choice.

The significant triple interaction effect indicates that the differential in the controller-other model imitation was greatest when the same-sex model mediated the positive reinforcers, and this effect was more pronounced for boys than for girls.

The data presented so far demonstrate that manipulation of

TABLE 2.2: *Summary of the Analysis of Variance of the Imitation Scores*

Source	df	MS	
Between subjects	47	310.17	
Sex of subjects (A)	1	283.59	<1
Sex of controller model (B)	1	128 34	<1
Adult versus child consumer (C)	1	518.01	1.61
A × B	1	23.01	<1
A × C	1	1.76	<1
B × C	1	742.59	2.31
A × B ×C	1	21.10	<1
Error (b)	40	321.49	
Within subjects	48	113.24	
Controller versus other model (D)	1	2,025.84	40.61***
A × D	1	297.51	5.96*
B × D	1	237.51	4.76*
C × D	1	396 09	7.94**
A × B × D	1	256.76	5.15*
A × C × D	1	19.52	<1
B × C × D	1	23.02	<1
A × B × C × D	1	184.00	3.69
Error (w)	40	49.88	

* $p < .05$.
** $p < .01$.
*** $p < .001$.

rewarding power had produced differential imitation of the behavior exhibited by the two models. In order to assess whether the dispensing of positive reinforcers in the prior social interaction influenced the overall level of matching responses, the imitation scores in each of the three groups were summed across models and analyzed using a Sex $\times$ Treatment design.

The mean total imitative responses for children in the Child Consumer, Adult Consumer, and the Control group were 50.21, 40.58, and 37.88, respectively. Analysis of variance of these data reveals a significant treatment effect ($F = 3.37, .025 < p < .05$). Further comparisons of pairs of means by the t test show that children in the child rewarded condition displayed significantly more imitative behavior than did children both in the Adult Consumer treatment ($t = 2.19, p < .05$), and those in the Control group ($t = 2.48, p < .02$). The Adult Consumer and Control groups, however, did not differ from each other in this respect ($t = .54$).

The model preference patterns were identical for children in the two experimental conditions and consequently, the data were combined for the statistical analysis. Of the 48 children, 32 selected the model who possessed rewarding power as the more attractive, while 16 perferred the noncontrolling adult. The greater attractiveness of the rewarding model was significant beyond the .05 level ($\chi^2 = 5.34$). The experimental triad in which boys were the recipients of positive reinforcers while the male model was ignored, and the female consumer-girl ignored subgroup, contributed the highest preference for the noncontrolling adult.

In addition to the experimental groups discussed in the preceding section, data are available for 9 children in the Adult Consumer condition, and for 11 children in the Child Consumer treatment who revealed, in their postexperiment interviews, that they had actually attributed rewarding power to the ignored or the consumer adult despite the elaborate experimental manipulations designed to establish differential power status. A number of these children were firmly convinced that only a male can possess resources and, therefore, the female dispensing the rewards was only an intermediary for the male model (for example, "He's the man and it's all his because he's a daddy. Mommy never really has things belong to her. . . . He's the daddy so it's his but he shares nice with the mommy. . . . He's the man and the man always really has the money and he lets ladies play too. John's good and polite and he has very good manners.") This view of resource ownership within the family constellation was often directly reinforced by the mothers (for example, "My mommy told me and Joan that the daddy really buys all the things, but the mommy looks after things."). Children who attributed the resource ownership to the consumer or ignored female model had considerable difficulty in explaining their selection (for example, "I just knowed it does. . . . I could tell, that's how."), perhaps, because the power structure they depicted is at variance with the widely accepted cultural norm.

As shown in Table 2.3, models who were attributed rewarding power elicited approximately twice as many matching responses as models who were perceived by the children as possessing no control over the rewarding resources. Because of the small and unequal number of cases in each cell, these data were not evaluated statistically. The differences, however, are marked and quite in accord with those produced by the experimentally manipulated variations in power status.

DISCUSSION

To the extent that the imitative behavior elicited in the present experiment may be considered an elementary prototype of identification within a nuclear family group, the data fail to support the interpretation of identificatory learning as the outcome of a rivalrous interaction between the child and the adult who occupies an envied status in respect to the consumption of highly desired resources. Children clearly identified with the source of rewarding power rather than with the competitor for these rewards. Moreover, power inversions on the part of the male and

TABLE 2.3: *Imitation as a Function of Attributed Rewarding Power to the Models*

Treatment condition	Objects of imitation			
	Female controller	Male noncontroller	Male controller	Female noncontroller
Adult consumer	24.0	12.3	29.8	14.6
Child consumer	18.2	6.7	35.5	16.2

female models produced cross-sex imitation, particularly in girls. The differential readiness of boys and girls to imitate behavior exhibited by an opposite-sex model are consistent with findings reported by Brown (1956, 1958) that boys show a decided preference for the masculine role, whereas, ambivalence and masculine role preference are widespread among girls. These findings probably reflect both the differential cultural tolerance for cross-sex behavior displayed by males and females, and the privileged status and relatively greater positive reinforcement of masculine role behavior in our society.

Failure to develop sex appropriate behavior has received considerable attention in the clinical literature and has customarily been assumed to be established and maintained by psychosexual threat and anxiety reducing mechanisms. Our findings strongly suggest, however, that external social learning variables, such as the distribution of rewarding power within the family constellation, may be highly influential in the formation of inverted sex role behavior.

Theories of identificatory learning have generally assumed that within the family setting the child's initial identification is confined to his mother, and that during early childhood boys must turn from the mother as the primary model to the father as the main source of imitative behavior. However, throughout the course of development children are provided with ample opportunities to observe the behavior of both parents. The results of the present experiment reveal that when children are exposed to multiple models they may select one or more of them as the primary source of behavior, but rarely reproduce all the elements of a single model's repertoire or confine their imitation to that model. Although the children adopted many of the characteristics of the model who possessed rewarding power, they also reproduced some of the elements of behavior exhibited by the model who occupied the subordinate role. Consequently, the children were not simply junior-size replicas of one or the other model; rather, they exhibited a relatively novel pattern of behavior representing an amalgam of elements from both models. Moreover, the specific admixture of behavioral elements varied from child to child. These findings provide considerable evidence for the seemingly paradoxical conclusion that imitation can in fact produce innovation of social behavior, and that within the same family even same-sex siblings may exhibit quite different response patterns, owing to their having selected for imitation different elements of their parents' response repertoires.

The association of a model with noncontingent positive reinforcement tends to increase the incidence of imitative behavior in two person groups (Bandura & Huston, 1961), whereas the addition of a same-sex third person who is denied access to desired rewards may provoke in children negative evaluations of the rewarding model and thereby decreases his potency as a modeling stimulus. These two sets of data demonstrate how learning principles based on an individual behavior model may be subject to strict limitations, since the introduction of additional social variables into the stimulus complex can produce significant changes in the functional relationships between relevant variables.

REFERENCES

BANDURA, A. 1962. Social learning through imitation. In M. R. Jones (Ed.), *Nebraska symposium on motivation: 1962.* Lincoln: University of Nebraska Press. Pp. 211–269.

BANDURA, A., & HUSTON, ALETHA C. 1961. Identification as a process of incidental learning. *Journal of Abnormal and Social Psychology,* 63, 311–318.

BRONFENBRENNER, U. 1960. Freudian theories of identification and their derivatives. *Child Development,* 31, 15–40.

BROWN, D. G. 1956. Sex-role preference in young children. *Psychological Monographs,* 70 (14, Whole No. 421).

FRENCH, J. R. P., JR., MORRISON, H. W., & LEVINGER, G. 1960. Coercive power and forces affecting conformity. *Journal of Abnormal and Social Psychology,* 61, 93–101.

FREUD, ANNA. 1946. *The ego and the mechanisms of defense.* New York: International University Press.

FREUD, S. 1924. The passing of the Oedipus-complex. In *Collected papers.* Vol. 2. London: Hogarth Press. Pp. 269–282.

FREUD, S. 1948. *Group psychology and the analysis of the ego.* London: Hogarth Press.

KAGAN, J. 1958. The concept of identification. *Psychological Review,* 65, 296–305.

KLEIN, MELANIE. 1949. *The psycho-analysis of children.* London: Hogarth Press.

MACCOBY, ELEANOR E. 1959. Role-taking in childhood and its consequences for social learning. *Child Development,* 30, 239–252.

MOWRER, O. H. 1950. Identification: A link between learning theory and psychotherapy. In *Learning theory and personality dynamics.* New York: Ronald Press. Pp. 69–94.

MOWRER, O. H. 1958. Hearing and speaking: An analysis of language learning. *Journal of Speech and Hearing Disorders,* 23, 143–152.

MUSSEN, P., & DISTLER, L. 1959. Masculinity, identification, and father-son relationships. *Journal of Abnormal and Social Psychology,* 59, 350–356.

PARSONS, T. 1955. Family structure and the socialization of the child. In T. Parsons & R. F. Bales (Eds.), *Family, socialization, and interaction process.* New York: The Free Press of Glencoe.

SEARS, R. R. 1957. Identification as a form of behavioral development. In D. B. Harris (Ed.), *The concept of development.* Minneapolis: University of Minnesota Press. Pp. 149–161.

WHITING, J. W. M. 1959. Sorcery, sin, and the superego: A cross-cultural study of some mechanisms of social control. In M. R. Jones (Ed.), *Nebraska symposium on motivation: 1959.* Lincoln: University of Nebraska Press. Pp. 174–195.

WHITING, J. W. M. 1960. Resource mediation and learning by identification. In I. Iscoe & H. W. Stevenson (Eds.), *Personality development in children.* Austin: University of Texas Press. Pp. 112–126.

ZIPF, SHEILA G. Resistance and conformity under the reward and punishment. *Journal of Abnormal and Social Psychology,* 61, 102–109.

3 Symbolic Coding Processes in Observational Learning

MARVIN D. GERST

It is increasingly evident from research on observational learning that modeling serves as one of the principal modes of acquiring new patterns of behavior. Although the phenomenon has been well documented empirically, the mechanisms governing observational learning have not been extensively investigated. In the theory recently proposed by Bandura (1969), observational learning is conceptualized as a multiprocess phenomenon encompassing (1) attentional processes that regulate

Reprinted by permission of the publisher from the JOURNAL OF PERSON-ALITY AND SOCIAL PSYCHOLOGY, 1971, Vol. 19, pp. 7–17. Copyright 1971, American Psychological Association.

This article is based on a doctoral dissertation presented to the Department of Psychology, Stanford University. The work was supported by a Public Health Service grant MH 05162 from the National Institute of Mental Health to Albert Bandura. Deep appreciation is expressed to my doctoral committee chairman Albert Bandura for his patience and skillful guidance, and to the committee members, Nathan Maccoby and Walter Mischel. Thanks also to Frederick J. McDonald, the Audio-Visual Division of the Stanford Department of Education for their generous loan of equipment, to Mrs. Lester Dutcher, an excellent model, and Jane Porter for non-specific support.

sensory registration of modeling stimuli; (2) retention processes that are influenced by rehearsal operations and symbolic coding of modeled events into easily remembered schemes; (3) motoric reproduction processes that are concerned with availability of component responses and the utilization of symbolic codes in guiding behavioral reproduction; and (4) incentive or motivational processes that determine whether or not acquired responses will be activated into overt performances. The present experiment was specifically designed to elucidate the role of symbolic coding activities in learning through observation of modeled behavior.

Under conditions in which observers do not overtly perform matching responses during the acquisition period, modeled responses can be acquired only in representational form. In the aforementioned theory, observational learning entails two representational systems, the imaginal and the verbal. It is assumed that during and after exposure to modeling stimuli, observers transform these events into symbolic forms and organize the essential elements into familiar and more easily remembered schemes. After modeled events have been coded into images or their verbal equivalents for memory representation they function as mediators for later response retrieval and reproduction.

The influence of symbolic representation in observational learning is shown in a study by Bandura, Grusec and Menlove (1966) who found that children generating verbal equivalents of modeled responses during a presentation later reproduced more matching responses than children who observed the modeled displays attentively without verbalization; the latter group in turn achieved a higher level of observational learning than those who engaged in symbolic activities designed to prevent implicit verbal coding of modeled behavior.

The above study provides some evidence that symbolic coding can enhance observational learning. It remains to be determined whether different coding systems vary in their relative efficacy. The utility of different coding operations may also depend partly upon the characteristics of the modeled responses. Verbal coding may be optimal for facilitating acquisition and retention of mod-

eled stimuli that can be easily described, whereas responses difficult to describe verbally may require a nonverbal coding operating, such as visualization. Moreover, symbolic codes that are
relatively easy to remember and to retrieve should be more
serviceable guides for delayed reproduction of modeled behavior
than codes that are difficult to retain.

The role played by symbolic activities in both learning and
memory has been the subject of increasing experimentation.
Miller (1956), who drew attention to coding processes some
years ago, proposed the unitization hypothesis according to
which individual items are categorized or organized into larger
coherent units or "chunks." He suggested that the process of
chunking or recoding into fewer but more informationally rich
categories is primarily verbal. Symbolic language allows one to
bring to bear on any set of stimuli a coding system which is already well learned and organized into a very large number of association networks. This system allows most information to be
coded into a mode which is easy to store and to retrieve. Depending on the nature of the stimuli and the necessity of veridi-
cal communication, the coding operation may be a process
shared by others (e.g., converting binary numbers into base 10
numbers) or idiosyncratic to the person, as when subjectively
meaningful but socially uninformative names are attached to a
set of shapes. Miller also suggested that the coding process need
not be exclusively verbal. It is possible that imagery may also
serve as a representational device.

Numerous investigations have shown that people do in fact re-
organize stimuli into larger inclusive categories and transform
them into symbolic systems that permit easy storage and retrieval. Retention of stimulus events is facilitated by organizational factors (Cofer, 1965; Lantz & Stefflre, 1964; Mandler,
1968; Tulving, 1966); verbal description of stimulus objects
generally aids in their retention (Kurtz & Hovland, 1953;
Ranken, 1963a, b; Glanzer & Clark, 1963a, b); and imagery can
substantially augment associative learning (Bower, 1969; Paivio,
1969).

In the present experiment adult subjects observed a filmed

model perform intricate motor responses varying in verbalizability. After each performance they engaged in one of the following symbolic activities: they described the specific movement and position elements in concrete terms (Verbal Description); they reinstated the modeled responses in vivid imagery (Imaginal Coding); they devised summary labels that encompassed the constituent elements in meaningful events (Summary Labeling); or they performed arithmetic calculations designed to impede symbolic coding of the modeling stimuli (Controls). The accuracy with which subjects reproduced the modeled responses was measured immediately after symbolic coding, and again following a delay period.

On the assumption that easily verbalized responses can also be easily visualized, it was hypothesized that the concrete description and visualization conditions would be superior to the control group without differing significantly from each other. However, for modeled responses that are difficult to describe verbally, it was predicted that subjects in the visualization condition would achieve better matching performances than those who coded the modeling stimuli into concrete descriptions of constituent elements.

The higher form of verbal code in which observers impose subjectively meaningful and abbreviated linguistic labels on complex modeling stimuli enables observers to organize diverse response elements efficiently in a form that can be easily stored, retained intact over long periods, and quickly retrieved. Since any modeled activity, however idosyncratic, can be likened to some meaningful object or event, the effectiveness of this type of coding operation should be relatively independent of the nature of the modeling stimuli. It was therefore predicted that subjects using summary labeling would achieve a higher level of observational learning of all types of modeled responses, and that they would retain significantly more matching behavior than subjects in the other treatment conditions.

METHOD

Subjects

The subjects were male and female college students drawn from the introductory psychology course and paid volunteers. A total of 72 subjects was randomly assigned to one of three experimental groups and a control condition of 18 subjects each. There were 35 males and 37 females with essentially equal sex distribution in the different groups.

Modeling Stimuli

The modeling stimuli that subjects observed and later reproduced were motoric responses drawn from the manual language of the deaf (Riekehof, 1963). Each modeled response, which consisted of intricate movements of the arms, hands, and fingers, was constructed by combining two manual words and performed as one continuous action. These types of responses were selected because novel behavioral patterns can be created by combining different movements, the responses vary in their susceptibility to verbal description, and members of a hearing population would never have encountered the particular sequences that were modeled.

Selection of Modeling Stimuli

Approximately 100 motoric responses varying in codability were performed twice each by a female teacher of the manual language. Verbal codability of the modeling stimuli was measured in terms of description accuracy. A group of 15 subjects observed each modeled response and described each aloud as concretely and as accurately as possible immediately after presentation. These descriptions were tape recorded and later rated independently for accuracy by two judges. Each response was analyzed into a predetermined set of movement and position elements for the purpose of scoring verbal codability. The judges rated the degree (from 0 to 3) to which described elements corresponded to those contained in the modeled responses. Interjudge reliability was high, the correlation coefficient being r = .88 for the responses included in the formal experiment.

Ten motoric responses were chosen on the basis of their verbal codability scores. Five of these responses, referred to as the Low Verbal (*LV*) set, were relatively difficult to describe accurately. The mean accuracy score for this set was 40% with a range of scores from 31–54%. The remaining five responses, designated as the High Verbal *(HV)* set, were chosen because they could be easily described in verbal terms, the mean accuracy being 69% with a range from 61–80%. Illustrative examples of responses in these two subgroups are provided in Figure 3.1.

The two sets of motoric items were then presented to ten additional subjects who were asked to reproduce each response be-

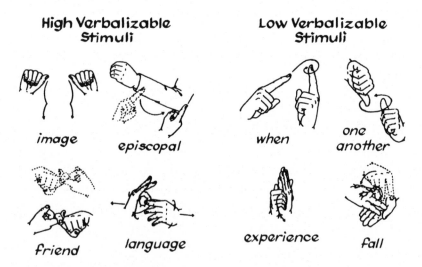

FIGURE 3.1. Examples of high and low verbalizable test stimuli employed

haviorally one minute after presentation. During the one-minute delay period subjects were required to count backwards by threes from a designated number. These data were collected to ensure that the response items were not so readily reproducible that there would be little possibility for the coding operations to exert an influence, nor so difficult as to preclude any improvement through coding. Low verbalizable responses were reproduced at a mean accuracy of 38%, with scores ranging from 23–35%. The accuracy scores for the *HV* set ranged from 42% to 81%, with a mean value of 66%. The modeled responses were thus demonstrated to be sufficiently difficult to permit the experimental procedures to exert an influence.

The ten motoric responses were recorded on black and white 16mm silent film. The model, who was photographed in a sitting position with only her torso visible, performed each response twice, with the break signaled by a brief dropping of the hands to her lap. Each sequence required 6 to 10 seconds to complete.

The film was organized with four practice items at the beginning, followed by the *HV* and *LV* responses presented in an alternating sequence. Each item was preceded by four seconds of black leader, and followed by one and one-half seconds of opaque leader and one second of black leader. The opaque leader warned the subject that the sequence was about to appear and the immediately following black leader was used to provide contrast for the lighter modeled displays.

Apparatus

The filmed responses were projected on a wall approximately 15 feet from the subject. The subject's behavioral reproductions were recorded on a remotely controlled MVR–15 video tape recorder located outside the experimental room. The video camera, equipped with a telephoto lens for close-in recording, was positioned facing the subject and at the same distance as the movie projector so as not to be intrusive. The subject's verbal productions were recorded simultaneously on the video tape and an independent audio tape recorder.

Experimental Sequence

Subjects were told that the experiment was concerned with the way people remember material presented visually. They were informed that they would be shown a series of modeled responses, one at a time, immediately after which they would be asked to engage in a designated symbolic activity for one minute. At the end of this period they would be asked to reproduce the modeled response as accurately as they could.

The four practice items were then presented in the same manner as the subsequent test items, except that subjects were again shown each modeled response after their behavioral reproduction was completed. This procedure allowed subjects to become familiar with the type of movements employed, and to gain some facility in utilizing the coding system that they would be required to employ with the experimental items.

Coding Procedures

SUMMARY LABELING

Subjects in this condition were instructed to develop summary labels that would encompass the constituent elements of the modeled movements in easily remembered form. Subjects were told that each movement or partial movement might call to mind some action or object of use in reminding them of the movement. They were further told that if a summary label or phrase did not come to mind they should try to construct one and continue to repeat it during the time provided, and that they could change labels during the one-minute coding period if they happened to think of one more fitting.

IMAGINAL CODING

Subjects in this group were told to close their eyes after the stimulus presentation and to visualize the modeled responses in vivid and detailed imagery. They were also instructed to continually reinstate these images during the entire one-minute coding period. In order to monitor their visualization activities, subjects were instructed to signal, by raising a finger, each time a modeled response was imaginally reactivated. In addition, after the acquisition test for each item, they rated the clarity of their visualization on a 7-point rating scale.

VERBAL DESCRIPTION

Subjects in this condition were instructed to describe aloud the specific movements and positions of the modeled responses as concretely and accurately as possible, and to continue to repeat these descriptions aloud throughout the one-minute post-exposure coding period. They were cautioned not to use analogies or similes such as "It looks like she is making a square," or "She seems to be covering a pot"—but rather to describe the responses in terms of exact movements and positions of the arms, hands and fingers.

CONTROLS

During the one-minute interval following exposure, subjects in the control group were required to count to the beat of a metronome either backward or forward by sevens or thirteens from numbers supplied by the experimenter. This cognitive activity was sufficiently demanding to prevent subjects from engaging in any symbolic coding, but sufficiently dissimilar to the modeled contents not to interfere with their retention.

Immediate Reproduction

The ten test items were presented one at a time. After a modeled response had been portrayed twice, the projector was stopped and the subject was instructed to engage in his assigned coding activities for one minute. He then reproduced the movements he had seen modeled while his performances were recorded on video tape. This procedure was repeated for each item.

Delayed Reproduction

After the ten items were completed, subjects were informed that they would be administered a different task ostensibly designed to measure their capacity to retain verbally presented material. The material employed was an essay describing the life and work of Gauss, "The Prince of Mathematicians" (Newman, 1956). They were instructed to read this essay aloud as rapidly as possible consistent with comprehension, and were informed that they would subsequently be asked questions about the material.

The choice of relatively complex verbal material and the announcement of a comprehension test were designed to concentrate the subject's attention on this distracting task and thus to prevent him from engaging in any symbolic rehearsal of the modeled responses during the delay period. In this way, the long-term retention of the modeled material could be measured without being confounded by unknown amounts of covert rehearsal.

Subjects engaged in this task for 15 minutes. At the end of this period they were asked to reproduce as many of the previously observed modeled responses as possible within three and one-half minutes. This time period was selected because it was found that pretest subjects exhausted the total number of responses they could perform within this interval. Subjects were informed that they could reproduce the responses in any order desired, utilizing the coding strategy previously employed to aid their recall, and that they should use the full three and one-half minute period to recall as many movements as possible. These performances were recorded on video tape for later scoring.

Scoring Procedure

Each modeled response was analyzed into its component elements, including the starting position of the fingers, hands, and arms, as well as their subsequent movements and final positions. For each response the scorable elements were noted and entered in the appropriate places on a master scoring grid. Each response was analyzed according to its separate elements, and a quantitative score was assigned to each "Position" element in terms of whether it was omitted (0), fragmentarily matched (1), substantially matched (2), or perfectly matched (3). Elements in the "Movement" column were assigned scores of either 0, 2, 4, or 6, depending upon the fidelity of the reproduction. These movement scores are twice the value of the position scores because it was considered desirable to weight the "Movement" and "Position" scores equally. The total number of points subjects received for each response was summed separately for the HV and LV items and divided by total possible points, to provide the percent behavioral reproduction scores.

Each of two judges rated reproductions of one-half the total sample, randomly drawn from each of the four experimental groups. In addition, they rated independently the same 20 protocols to assess inter-judge reliability. The judges scored the immediate reproductions with reliability of $r = +.90$ for the HV items, and $r = +.91$ for the LV items. The corresponding relia-

TABLE 3.1: *Mean Percent of Modeled Responses Reproduced as a Function of Coding Activity, Verbalizability of the Modeled Responses, and Time-Reproduction Test*

	Immediate		Delay		
	HV*	LV**	HV	LV	Overall Means
Summary Labeling	78.86	72.18	43.22	42.82	59.27
Imaginal Coding	81.43	72.05	41.76	28.31	55.89
Verbal Description	74.54	60.19	38.40	29.61	50.68
Control	61.74	53.89	35.51	22.98	43.53
Overall Means	74.14	64.58	39.72	30.93	
	69.36		35.33		

* HV = High Verbalizable items
** LV = Low Verbalizable items

bility coefficients for their scoring of delayed reproduction was r = +.92 and r = +.96 for the *HV* and *LV* items, respectively.

Results

Data for males and females were pooled since tests revealed no significant differences on any of the dependent measures. Table 3.2 presents the mean percent of modeled responses that were reproduced by subjects in the different treatment conditions.

Results of the analysis of variance performed on these data disclosed that the main effects of treatment conditions (F =

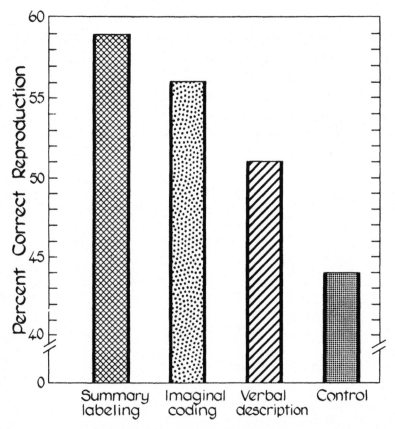

FIGURE 3.2. Total percentage reproduction scores for all groups

11.47; $p < .001$), time of the reproduction test (F = 726.35; $p < .001$), and verbalizability (F = 41.83; $p < .001$) were highly significant sources of variance. In addition, it was found that the treatment conditions had a differential effect depending upon the time at which the test for behavioral reproduction was conducted (F = 4.49; $p < .01$). However, the hypothesized interaction between type of coding activity and verbalizability of the modeled responses did not emerge as a significant source of variance (F = 1.57). These findings are discussed separately below.

Symbolic Coding Effects

The treatment effects are presented graphically in Figure 3.2. Comparisons of pairs of treatment conditions by the *t*-test revealed that subjects in the Summary Labeling condition did not differ from the Imaginal Coding group, but the Labeling group did achieve superior reproduction when compared to subjects who utilized Verbal Description ($t = 4.22$; p $< .001$) and those in the Control group ($t = 7.74$; $p < .001$). Imaginal Coding was likewise superior to Verbal Description ($t = 2.56$; $p < .02$) and to the performance of the Controls ($t = 6.08$; $p < .001$). Subjects who used Verbal Description achieved a higher level of observational learning than the Controls ($t = 3.52$; $p < .01$).

Time of Reproduction

All groups performed significantly more matching behaviors one minute after exposure than following a 15-minute interval during which they could not rehearse previously learned modeled responses. The immediate reproduction score for all groups combined was 69.36%, whereas subjects were able to perform only 35.33% of previously modeled behavior during the delayed test. This temporal variable was involved in a significant two-way interaction and will be discussed more fully later.

Verbalizability

As might be expected, all groups acquired and retained significantly more easily the modeled responses that could be verbally described than those not readily subject to verbal coding. The degrees of reproduction of high and low verbalizable responses were 56.93% and 47.76%, respectively. In the delayed recall period, all groups except the Summary Labeling group show significantly less retention of low verbalizable than high verbalizable responses. The t values for these comparisons were as follows: Summary Labeling, $t<1$; Verbal Description, $t = 6.67$; Imaginal Coding, $t = 10.21$; Control, $t = 9.51$. However, since the three-way interaction was not of statistically significant magnitude, these differences can only be considered as suggestive evidence that coding in summary labeling form enables observers to retain both difficult and easily verbalized material equally well. It would be desirable to examine this phenomenon further in future investigations.

Interaction Effect of Coding and Temporal Factors

Figure 3.3 presents graphically the significant two-way interaction between treatment conditions and the time of behavioral reproduction, indicating that the coding operations employed in the present investigation are differentially powerful when behavioral reproduction is attempted shortly after exposure and after a delay of some length.

In order to determine which differences contributed to the significant interaction, pairs of conditions were compared separately with regard to immediate and delayed reproduction scores. Intergroup comparisons on matching performances in the immediate reproduction test yielded the following pattern of differences: Summary Labeling and Imaginal Coding groups did not differ from each other ($t < 1$). Subjects in the Summary Labeling condition achieved higher reproduction scores than those in the

Verbal Description group ($t = 2.41$; $p < .05$) and the Control group (t $= 5.23$; $p < .001$). Similarly, subjects who employed Imaginal Coding were superior to the Verbal Description group ($t = 2.77$; $p < .01$) and the Controls ($t = 5.51$; $p < .001$). And finally, the Verbal Description group exceeded the Controls ($t = 2.82$; $p < .01$) in accuracy of matching behavior.

In the delayed reproduction test, however, the Summary Labeling group retained more of the observed behaviors than sub-

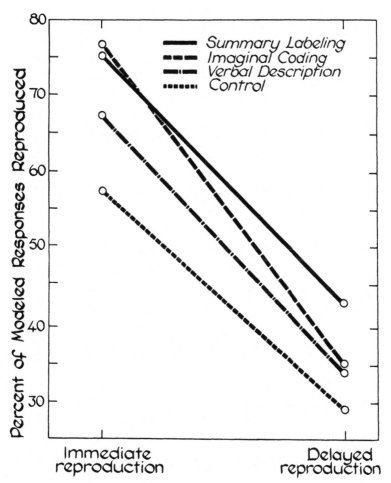

FIGURE 3.3.   Acquisition and delayed reproduction of modeled responses as a function of symbolic coding activities

jects in the Imaginal Coding group ($t = 2.36$; $p < .05$), in the Verbal Description condition ($t = 2.66$; $p < .02$), or in the Control group ($t = 4.07$; $p < .001$). The latter three groups did not differ significantly from one another. The magnitude of the decrement from immediate to delayed reproduction for the Imaginal Coding group compared to that of the other groups showed this coding operation to be the most vulnerable to temporal loss ($t = 4.41$; $p < .001$).

Integrated Reproduction of Modeled Responses

It was assumed that coding of modeled responses into meaningful summary labels facilitates observational learning because such memory codes organize diverse elements of a modeled display into an easily stored form. Consequently, appropriate responses can be more easily retrieved from this type of memory code than from representational systems that rely on the coding of individual elements. This assumption was tested by tabulating the number of modeled responses that subjects in the different treatment conditions were able to reproduce accurately at the delayed test in complete integrated form, that is, containing all the elements enacted in the correct sequence.

The mean numbers of responses reproduced in their entirety for the different treatment conditions were: Summary Labeling = 4.17; Imaginal Coding = 1.83; Verbal Description = 1.44; Control = 1.94. Analysis of variance of these data revealed a significant treatment effect ($F = 9.76$; $p < .01$). In intergroup comparisons the Labeling treatment was significantly different (beyond the .001 level) from each of the other conditions, which did not differ from each other.

It is conceivable that the above differences might have been influenced by the total amount of modeled behavior retained. Therefore, to examine this possibility the percentage of the total items reproduced in the delayed test that were of well-integrated form was calculated. The mean percentages for the different treatment conditions were as follows: Summary Labeling =

63%; Imaginal Coding = 37%; Verbal Description = 27%; Control = 42%. Analysis of variance performed on these scores yielded a highly significant difference (F = 67.63; $p < .001$). As in the previous analysis, the Labeling condition differed significantly from the other groups, which did not differ significantly from each other.

Labeling at Delayed Reproduction

During the delayed reproduction test none of the subjects in the Verbal Description condition could recall their concrete descriptions of the modeled responses, while all Labeling subjects were able to recall their summary codes for at least some of the modeled items. To test whether retention of summary codes facilitates delayed behavioral reproduction, matching scores were compared between items for which summary codes were and were not retained. Modeled responses for which subjects could produce the summary codes were performed at a much higher level of accuracy (52%) than those for which the code was lost (7%), a difference that is highly significant ($t = 11.52$; $p < .001$).

Clarity of Imagery and Behavioral Reproduction

One would expect that clarity of imagery and behavioral reproduction would be positively related, since vivid imaginal representation provides a better guide for subsequent behavioral reproduction. To test this product-moment correlations were computed between ratings of the clarity with which imagery was achieved and behavioral reproductions at immediate and delayed time periods. It can be seen from the correlations presented in Table 3.2 that the hypothesized relationship received some support. Imaginal clarity and accuracy of reproduction are positively correlated, although only two of the coefficients are of statistically significant magnitude. The benefits of vivid imagery are most apparent with modeled responses that are difficult to code verbally (clarity vs. immediate low reproduction) and in retention of previously acquired modeled responses (clarity vs. delayed reproduction).

DISCUSSION

Findings of the present experiment provide evidence for the hypothesis that symbolic coding operations play an important role in observational learning. All three coding systems investigated facilitated initial behavioral reproduction compared to the performance of subjects who had no opportunity to code the modeling stimuli.

The hypothesis that summary labeling would prove superior to the other coding systems also received qualified support. Although the summary labeling and imaginal conditions did not differ in immediate response reproduction, subjects in the former group achieved a higher level of response acquisition than did the verbal description and the control groups. Moreover, subjects who coded the modeling stimuli into meaningful concise labels retained significantly more modeled responses overall than subjects in all other conditions.

TABLE 3.2: *Correlations Between Measures of Vividness of Imagery and Behavioral Reproduction Scores*

Imaginal Coding (N = 18)	r
Mean Clarity *vs* Immediate Reproduction	.31
Mean Clarity *vs* Delayed Reproduction	.42*
Mean Clarity *(LV) vs* Immediate Low Mean Reproduction	.43*
Mean Clarity *(HV) vs* Immediate High Mean Reproduction	.08
Mean Clarity *(LV) vs* Delayed Low Mean Reproduction	.24
Mean Clarity *(HV) vs* Delayed High Mean Reproduction	.28

* $p < .05$

The relative superiority of the summary labeling scheme is shown even more clearly when matching performances are scored according to a stringent criterion requiring all the response elements to be reproduced in the exact sequence in which they were originally modeled. Subjects who coded the modeling stimuli into concise labels were able to reproduce approximately twice as many well-integrated responses in the retention test as compared to the matching performances of the other groups. As noted previously, the efficacy of summary codes is most likely attributable to the fact that they permit observers to organize relatively complex stimuli into meaningful, concise, and easily remembered verbal codes. Consequently, modeled responses can be conveniently stored in this form and later used to reproduce the corresponding responses.

When persons represent relatively meaningless patterns of stimulation in terms of meaningful activities or familiar objects, the concise label is also likely to evoke relevant imagery. Subjects may therefore utilize both verbal and visual guides for later motoric reproduction. The imagery producing effects of stimulation may also partly explain why control subjects were able to achieve some acquisition and retention of modeled contents. Although subjects in this group were prevented from coding the modeling stimuli into verbal forms, they nevertheless may have utilized imaginal residues of the initial external stimulation. It would be of considerable interest to study observational learning under conditions where the development of both verbal and imaginal representations of modeling stimuli is effectively impeded.

It is noteworthy that imagery proved superior to concrete verbalization in facilitating observational learning. This finding may be interpreted in several ways. Perhaps modeled responses can be more easily and frequently reinstated imaginally than they can be described verbally. To check this possibility, the number of times imaginal subjects visualized the modeled responses and the verbalization subjects described the responses was scored. For the imaginal coding group, the mean number of visualizations was 11.1. For the verbal description group the mean number of descriptive repetitions was 2.8. The difference between these means is highly significant ($t = 8.10$; $p < .001$). A second possible interpretation is that imagery reinstates modeled responses in a more organized and integrated form, whereas concrete verbalization restores the responses in a fragmentary fashion. More frequent and better organized representation of modeled events would aid in their acquisition. Whatever the explanation may be, the findings of this study provide further evidence for the influential role of imaginal mediators in learning processes.

The results of this study failed to support the subsidiary hypothesis that the efficacy of different coding systems would partly depend on the ease with which the modeled responses could be described verbally. While the descriptive properties of modeled responses affected observational learning, imagery did not emerge as superior with non-verbalizable responses and conversely, verbal encoding did not prove most effective with highly describable responses. Two factors may be operative here. First, different criteria for categorizing responses and a wider range of values may be required to determine whether these findings are attributable to problems of item selection. Second, it may be that verbalizability and visualizability of the responses employed are positively correlated; that is, modeled responses that are easy to describe may also be easy to visualize.

To test this hypothesis, the mean number of visualizations and the mean clarity of the visualizations reported by subjects in the imaginal condition were compared for high and low verbalizable items. Results of this analysis show that *HV* items were visualized more often ($X = 11.87$) than *LV* items ($X = 10.41$), a difference that is highly significant ($t = 3.48$; $p < .01$). A comparable analysis of the clarity with which the two sets of modeled behaviors were visualized revealed that subjects visualized the *HV* items ($X = 2.80$) more vividly than they did the *LV* items ($X = 2.01$). This difference is also highly significant ($t = 6.13$; $p < .001$).

The preceding findings suggest that imaginal and verbal coding could be similarly affected by the item properties, but on the basis of the operation of different processes. A definitive test of the predicted interaction effect between item verbalizability and type of coding system would, therefore, require the use of high verbalizable items that evoke weak imagery, and low verbalizable items that produce high and vivid imagery.

The hypothesis that the summary labeling code would prove to be superior for memory reproduction was partially corroborated. However, subjects in all groups displayed a substantial loss of modeled responses after a period in which their attention was focused on entirely different activities. This response decrement probably reflects the operation of at least three factors. First, the modeled responses were relatively meaningless which would hinder both acquisition and retention. Second, the different responses were composed of various combinations of a relatively small set of common elements. Such high commonality of component responses can have deleterious effects on retention processes through associative interference. In the acquisition phase, of course, associative interference was minimal because the responses were reproduced one at a time in sequential modeling trials, whereas in the delayed test the various responses could be easily confused. Finally, subjects were prevented from rehearsing what they had learned, the process by which individuals ordinarily stabilize and strengthen acquired responses.

It is interesting that clarity of imagery was positively associated with reproduction of low verbalizable responses immediately following exposure, and with reproduction of both classes of responses in the delayed test. These relationships provide further suggestive evidence that subjects in the imaginal coding condition were engaging in imaginal activities and that these activities had a functional relationship to observational learning.

The findings of the present experiment also have bearing on nonmediational theories of imitative learning. The Skinnerian analysis of modeling phenomena (Baer & Sherman, 1964; Baer, Peterson, & Sherman, 1967; Skinner, 1957) assumes that modeled behavior is acquired as a result of differential reinforcement of matching responses. This analysis of modeling phenomena does not distinguish between acquisition and performance since it is believed that the acquisition process cannot be directly observed and is thus fruitless to investigate. In a recent paper, Gewirtz and Stingle (1968) assert that mediational processes can only be inferred from the very behavior they are purported to explain, so that one gains no new information from such an analysis. This criticism might be valid when applied to theories that postulate hypothetical internal constructs as the major determinants of overt behavior. In the present study, however, the symbolic activities were independently manipulated rather than inferred from motor matching responses which constituted the dependent events. Results of this experiment and related studies discussed in the introductory sections demonstrate that symbolic activities are not only manipulable, but can exercise strong influence over behavior.

The findings of this study further illustrate the need to analyze the variables governing observational learning, the effects of which occur before any matching responses are performed. After responses are acquired observationally, reinforcement variables may play a decisive role in regulating the performance of matching responses. An adequate theory of modeling must account not only for the appearance of matching behavior, but also for the absence of matching behavior following exposure to modeling stimuli, for the specificity of matching performances, and for variations in retention of modeled behavior. A multi-process theory that encompasses attentional, coding and organization, and motivational processes, would pherhaps be best suited to account for modeling phenomena.

R E F E R E N C E S

BAER, D. M., & SHERMAN, J. A. 1964. Reinforcement control of generalized imitation in young children. *Journal of Experimental Child Psychology,* 1, 37–49.

BAER, D. M., PETERSON, R. F., & SHERMAN, J. A. 1967. The development of imitation by reinforcing behavioral similarity to a model. *Journal of the Experimental Analysis of Behavior,* 10, 405–416.

BANDURA, A. 1969. *Principles of behavior modification.* New York: Holt, Rinehart & Winston.

BANDURA, A., GRUSEC, J. E., & MENLOVE, F. L. 1966. Observational learning as a function of symbolization and incentive set. *Child Development,* 37, 499–506.

BOWER, G. 1969. Mental imagery and associative learning. In L. Gregg (Ed.), *Cognition in learning and memory.* New York: Wiley.

COFER, C. N. 1965. On some factors in the organizational characteristics of free recall. *American Psychologist,* 20, 261–272.

EDWARDS, A. L. 1960. *Statistical methods for the behavioral sciences.* New York: Holt, Rinehart & Winston.

GEWIRTZ, J. L., & STINGLE, K. 1968. Learning of generalized imitation as the basis for identification. *Psychological Review,* 75, 374–397.

GLANZER, M., & CLARK, W. H. 1963a. Accuracy of perceptual recall: An analysis of organization. *Journal of Verbal Learning and Verbal Behavior,* 1, 289–299.

GLANZER, M., & CLARK, W. H. 1963b. The verbal loop hypothesis: Binary numbers. *Journal of Verbal Learning and Verbal Behavior,* 2, 301–309.

KURTZ, K., & HOVLAND, C. I. 1953. The effect of verbalization during observation of stimulus objects upon accuracy of recognition and recall. *Journal of Experimental Psychology,* 45, 157–164.

LANTZ, D., & STEFFLRE, V. 1964. Language and cognition revisited. *Journal of Abnormal and Social Psychology,* 69, 472–481.

MANDLER, G. 1968. Association and organization: Facts, fancies, and theories. In T. R. Dixon & D. L. Horton (Eds.), *Verbal behavior and general behavior theory.* Englewood Cliffs, N. J.: Prentice-Hall. Pp. 109–119.

MILLER, G. A. 1956. The magical number seven, plus or minus two: Some limits on our capacity for processing information. *Psychological Review,* 63, 81–97.

NEWMAN, J. (Ed.) 1956. *The world of mathematics.* New York: Simon and Schuster. Vol. 1–IV.

PAIVIO, A. 1969. Mental imagery in associative learning and memory. *Psychological Review,* 76, 241–263.

RANKEN, H. B. 1963a. Language and thinking: Positive and negative effects of naming. *Science,* 141, 48–50.

RANKEN, H. B. 1963b. Effects of name learning on serial learning, position learning, and recognition learning with random shapes. *Psychological Reports,* 13, 663–678.

RIEKEHOF, L. 1963. *Talk to the deaf.* Springfield, Ill.: Gospel Publishing House.

SKINNER, B. F. 1957. *Verbal behavior.* New York: Appleton-Century-Crofts.

TULVING, E. 1966. Subjective organization and effects of repetition in multi-trial free recall learning. *Journal of Verbal Learning and Verbal Behavior,* 5, 193–197.

4

Influence of Models' Reinforcement Contingencies on the Acquisition of Imitative Responses

ALBERT BANDURA

It is widely assumed that the occurrence of imitative or observational learning is contingent on the administration of reinforcing stimuli either to the model or to the observer. According to the theory propounded by Miller and Dollard (1941), for example, the necessary conditions for learning through imitation include a motivated subject who is positively reinforced for matching the rewarded behavior of a model during a series of initially random, trial-and-error responses. Since this conceptualization of observational learning requires the sub-

Reprinted by permission of the publisher from the JOURNAL OF PERSON-ALITY AND SOCIAL PSYCHOLOGY, 1965, Vol. 1, pp. 589–595. Copyright 1965, American Psychological Association.

This investigation was supported by Research Grant M-5162 from the National Institutes of Health, United States Public Health Service. The author is indebted to Carole Revelle who assisted in collecting the data.

ject to perform the imitative response before he can learn it, this theory evidently accounts more adequately for the emission of previously learned matching responses, than for their acquisition.

Mowrer's (1960) proprioceptive feedback theory similarly highlights the role of reinforcement but, unlike Miller and Dollard who reduce imitation to a special case of instrumental learning, Mowrer focuses on the classical conditioning of positive and negative emotions to matching response-correlated stimuli. Mowrer distinguishes two forms of imitative learning in terms of whether the observer is reinforced directly or vicariously. In the former case, the model performs a response and simultaneously rewards the observer. If the modeled responses are thus paired repeatedly with positive reinforcement they gradually acquire secondary reward value. The observer can then administer positively conditioned reinforcers to himself simply by reproducing as closely as possible the model's positively valenced behavior. In the second, or empathetic form of imitative learning, the model not only exhibits the responses but also experiences the reinforcing consequences. It is assumed that the observer, in turn, experiences empathetically both the response-correlated stimuli and the response consequences of the model's behavior. As a result of this higher-order vicarious conditioning, the observer will be inclined to reproduce the matching responses.

There is some recent evidence that imitative behavior can be enhanced by noncontingent social reinforcement from a model (Bandura & Huston, 1961), by response-contingent reinforcers administered to the model (Bandura, Ross, & Ross, 1963b; Walters, Leat, & Mezei, 1963), and by increasing the reinforcing value of matching responses per se through direct reinforcement of the participant observer (Baer & Sherman, 1964). Nevertheless, reinforcement theories of imitation fail to explain the learning of matching responses when the observer does not perform the model's responses during the process of acquisition, and for which reinforcers are not delivered either to the model or to the observers (Bandura et al., 1961, 1963a).

The acquisition of imitative responses under the latter conditions appears to be accounted for more adequately by a contiguity theory of observational learning. According to the latter conceptualization (Bandura, 1965; Sheffield, 1961), when an observer witnesses a model exhibit a sequence of responses the observer acquires, through contiguous association of sensory events, perceptual and symbolic responses possessing cue properties that are capable of eliciting, at some time after a demonstration, overt responses corresponding to those that had been modeled.

Some suggestive evidence that the *acquisition* of matching responses may take place through contiguity, whereas reinforcements administered to a model exert their major influence on the *performance* of imitatively learned responses, is provided in a study in which models were rewarded or punished for exhibiting aggressive behavior (Bandura et al., 1963b). Although children who had observed aggressive responses rewarded subsequently reproduced the model's behavior while children in the model-punished condition failed to do so, a number of the subjects in the latter group described in postexperimental interviews the model's repertoire of aggressive responses with considerable accuracy. Evidently, they had learned the cognitive equivalents of the model's responses but they were not translated into their motoric forms. These findings highlighted both the importance of distinguishing between learning and performance and the need for a systematic study of whether reinforcement is primarily a learning-related or a performance-related variable.

In the present experiment children observed a film-mediated model who exhibited novel physical and verbal aggressive responses. In one treatment condition the model was severely punished; in a second, the model was generously rewarded; while the third condition presented no response consequences to the model. Following a postexposure test of imitative behavior, children in all three groups were offered attractive incentives contingent on their reproducing the models' responses so as to provide a more accurate index of learning. It was predicted that reinforcing consequences to the model would result in significant differences in the performance of imitative behavior with the model-rewarded group displaying the highest number of different classes of matching responses, followed by the no-consequences and the model-punished groups, respectively. In accordance with previous findings (Bandura et al., 1961, 1963a) it was also expected that boys would perform significantly more imitative aggression than girls. It was predicted, however, that the introduction of positive incentives would wipe out both reinforcement-produced and sex-linked performance differences, revealing an equivalent amount of learning among children in the three treatment conditions.

METHOD

Subjects

The subjects were 33 boys and 33 girls enrolled in the Stanford University Nursery School. They ranged in age from 42 to 71 months, with a mean age of 51 months. The children were assigned randomly to one of three treatment conditions of 11 boys and 11 girls each.

Two adult males served in the role of models, and one female experimenter conducted the study for all 66 children.

Exposure Procedure

The children were brought individually to a semidarkened room. The experimenter informed the child that she had some business to attend to before they could proceed to the "surprise playroom," but that during the waiting period the child might watch a televised program. After the child was seated, the experimenter walked over to the television console, ostensibly tuned in a program and then departed. A film of approximately 5 minutes duration depicting the modeled responses was shown on a glass lenscreen in the television console by means of a rear projection arrangement, screened from the child's view by large panels. The televised form of presentation was utilized primarily because attending responses to televised stimuli are strongly conditioned in children and this procedure would therefore serve to enhance observation which is a necessary condition for the occurrence of imitative learning.

The film began with a scene in which the model walked up to an adult-size plastic Bobo doll and ordered him to clear the way. After glaring for a moment at the noncompliant antagonist the model exhibited four novel aggressive responses each accompanied by a distinctive verbalization.

First, the model laid the Bobo doll on its side, sat on it, and punched it in the nose while remarking, "Pow, right in the nose, boom, boom." The model then raised the doll and pommeled it on the head with a mallet. Each response was accompanied by the verbalization, "Sockeroo . . . stay down." Following the mallet aggression, the model kicked the doll about the room, and these responses were interspersed with the comment, "Fly away." Finally, the model threw rubber balls at the Bobo doll, each strike punctuated with "Bang." This sequence of physically and verbally aggressive behavior was repeated twice.

The component responses that enter into the development of more complex novel patterns of behavior are usually present in children's behavioral repertoires as products either of maturation or of prior social learning. Thus, while most of the elements in the modeled acts had undoubtedly been previously learned, the particular pattern of components in each response, and their evocation by specific stimulus objects, were relatively unique. For example, children can manipulate objects, sit on them, punch them, and they can make vocal responses, but the likelihood that a given child would spontaneously place a Bobo doll on its side, sit on it, punch it in the nose and remark, "Pow . . . boom, boom," is exceedingly remote. Indeed, a previous study utilizing the same stimulus objects has shown that the imitative responses selected for the present experiment have virtually a zero probability of occurring spontaneously among pre-school children (Bandura et al., 1961) and, therefore, meet the criterion of novel responses.

The rewarding and punishing contingencies associated with the model's aggressive responses were introduced in the closing scene of the film.

For children in the model-rewarded condition, a second adult appeared with an abundant supply of candies and soft drinks. He informed the model that he was a "strong champion" and that his superb aggressive performance clearly deserved a generous treat. He then poured him a large glass of 7-Up, and readily supplied additional energy-building nourishment including chocolate bars, Cracker Jack popcorn, and an assortment of candies. While the model was rapidly consuming the delectable treats, his admirer symbolically reinstated the modeled aggressive responses and engaged in considerable positive social reinforcement.

For children in the model-punished condition, the reinforcing agent appeared on the scene shaking his finger menacingly and commenting reprovingly, "Hey there, you big bully. You quit picking on that clown. I won't tolerate it." As the model drew back he tripped and fell, the other adult sat on the model and spanked him with a rolled-up magazine while reminding him of his aggressive behavior. As the model ran off cowering, the agent forewarned him, "If I catch you doing that again, you big bully, I'll give you a hard spanking. You quit acting that way."

Children in the no-consequences condition viewed the same film as shown to the other two groups except that no reinforcement ending was included.

Performance Measure

Immediately following the exposure session the children were escorted to an experimental room that contained a Bobo doll, three balls, a mallet and pegboard, dart guns, cars, plastic farm animals, and a doll house equipped with furniture and a doll family. By providing a variety of stimulus objects the children were at liberty to exhibit imitative responses or to engage in non-imitative forms of behavior.

After the experimenter instructed the child that he was free to play with the toys in the room, she excused herself supposedly to fetch additional play materials. Since many preschool children are reluctant to remain alone and tend to leave after a short period of time, the experimenter reentered the room midway through the session and reassured the child that she would return shortly with the goods.

Each child spent 10 minutes in the test room during which time his behavior was recorded every 5 seconds in terms of predetermined imitative response categories by judges who observed the session through a one-way mirror in an adjoining observation room.

Two observers shared the task of recording the occurrence of matching responses for all 66 children. Neither of the raters had knowledge of the treatment conditions to which the children were assigned. In order to provide an estimate of interscorer reliability, the responses of 10 children were scored independently by both observers. Since the imitative responses were highly distinctive and required no subjective interpretation, the raters were virtually in perfect agreement (99%) in scoring the matching responses.

The number of different physical and verbal imitative responses emitted spontaneously by the children constituted the performance measure.

Acquisition Index

At the end of the performance session the experimenter entered the room with an assortment of fruit juices in a colorful juice-dispensing fountain, and booklets of sticker-pictures that were employed as the positive incentives to activate into performance what the children had learned through observation.

After a brief juice treat the children were informed, that for each physical or verbal imitative response that they reproduced, they would receive a pretty sticker-picture and additional juice treats. An achievement incentive was also introduced in order to produce further disinhibition and to increase the children's motivation to exhibit matching responses. The experimenter attached a pastoral scene to the wall and expressed an interest in seeing how many sticker-pictures the child would be able to obtain to adorn his picture.

The experimenter then asked the child, "Show me what Rocky did in the TV program," "Tell me what he said," and rewarded him immediately following each matching response. If a child simply described an imitative response he was asked to give a performance demonstration.

Although learning must be inferred from performance, it was assumed that the number of different physical and verbal imitative responses reproduced by the children under the positive-incentive conditions would serve as a relatively accurate index of learning.

RESULTS

Figure 4.1 shows the mean number of different matching responses reproduced by children in each of the three treatment conditions during the no-incentive and the positive-incentive phases of the experiment. A squareroot transformation ($y = \sqrt{f} + \frac{1}{2}$) was applied to these data to make them amenable to parametric statistical analyses.

Performance Differences

A summary of the analysis of variance based on the performance scores is presented in Table 4.1. The findings reveal that reinforcing consequences to the model had a significant effect on the number of matching responses that the children spontaneously reproduced. The main effect of sex is also highly significant, confirming the prediction that boys would perform more imitative responses than girls.

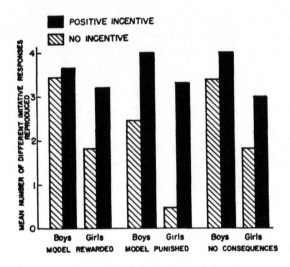

FIGURE 4.1.   Mean number of different matching responses reproduced by children as a function of positive incentives
and the model's reinforcement contingencies

Further comparisons of pairs of means by *t* tests (Table 4.2)
show that while the model-rewarded and the no-consequences
groups did not differ from each other, subjects in both of these
conditions performed significantly more matching responses than
children who had observed the model experience punishing consequences following the display of aggression. It is evident, however, from the differences reported separately for boys and girls
in Table 4.2, that the significant effect of the model's reinforcement contingencies is based predominantly on differences among
the girls' subgroups.*

Differences In Acquisition

An analysis of variance of the imitative learning scores is summarized in Table 4.3. The introduction of positive incentives

* Because of the skewness of the distribution of scores for the subgroup
of girls in the model-punished condition, differences involving this group
were also evaluated by means of the Mann-Whitney *U* test. The nonparametric analyses yield probability values that are identical to those reported in Table 2.

TABLE 4.1: *Analysis of Variance of Imitative Performance Scores*

Source	df	MS	F
Treatments (T)	2	1.21	3.27*
Sex (S)	1	4.87	13.16**
T × S	2	.12	<1
Within groups	60	.37	

* p <.05.
** p <.001.

completely wiped out the previously observed performance differences, revealing an equivalent amount of imitative learning among the children in the model-rewarded, model-punished, and the no-consequences treatment groups. Although the initially large sex difference was substantially reduced in the positive-incentive condition, the girls nevertheless still displayed fewer matching responses than the boys.

Acquisition Performance Differences

In order to elucidate further the influence of direct and vicariously experienced reinforcement on imitation, the differences in matching responses displayed under nonreward and positive-incentive conditions for each of the three experimental treatments were evaluated by the *t*-test procedure for correlated means. Table 4.4 shows that boys who witnessed the model either re-

TABLE 4.2: *Comparison of Pairs of Means between Treatment Conditions*

Performance measure	Treatment conditions		
	Reward versus punishment	Reward versus no consequences	Punishment versus no consequences
	t	*t*	*t*
Total sample	2.20**	0.55	2.25**
Boys	1.05	0.19	1.24
Girls	2.13**	0.12	2.02*

* p <.05.
** p <.025.

TABLE 4.3: *Analysis of Variance of Imitative Learning Scores*

Source	df	MS	F
Treatments (T)	2	0.02	<1
Sex (S)	1	0.56	6.22*
T × S	2	0.02	<1
Within groups	60	0.09	

* $p < .05$.

warded or left without consequences performed all of the imitative responses that they had learned through observation and no new matching responses emerged when positive reinforcers were made available. On the other hand, boys who had observed the model punished and girls in all three treatment conditions showed significant increments in imitative behavior when response-contingent reinforcement was later introduced.

DISCUSSION

The results of the present experiment lend support to a contiguity theory of imitative learning; reinforcements administered to the model influenced the observers' performance but not the acquisition of matching responses.

It is evident from the findings, however, that mere exposure to modeling stimuli does not provide sufficient conditions for imita-

TABLE 4.4: *Significance of the Acquisition-Performance Differences in Imitative Responses*

	Treatment conditions		
Group	Reward	Punishment	No consequences
	t	t	t
Total sample	2.38*	5.00***	2.67**
Boys	0.74	2.26*	1.54
Girls	3.33**	5.65***	2.18*

* $p < .025$.
** $p < .01$.
*** $p < .001$.

tive or observational learning. The fact that most of the children in the experiment failed to reproduce the entire repertoire of behavior exhibited by the model, even under positive-incentive conditions designed to disinhibit and to elicit matching responses, indicates that factors other than mere contiguity of sensory stimulation undoubtedly influence imitative response acquisition.

Exposing a person to a complex sequence of stimulation is no guarantee that he will attend to the entire range of cues, that he will necessarily select from a total stimulus complex only the most relevant stimuli, or that he will even perceive accurately the cues to which his attention is directed. Motivational variables, prior training in discriminative observation, and the anticipation of positive or negative reinforcements contingent on the emission of matching responses may be highly influential in channeling, augmenting, or reducing observing responses, which is a necessary precondition for imitative learning (Bandura, 1962; Bandura & Walters, 1963). Procedures that increase the distinctiveness of the relevant modeling stimuli also greatly facilitate observational learning (Sheffield & Maccoby, 1961).

In addition to attention-directing variables, the rate, amount, and complexity of stimuli presented to the observer may partly determine the degree of imitative learning. The acquisition of matching responses through observation of a lengthy uninterrupted sequence of behavior is also likely to be governed by principles of associated learning such as frequency and recency, serial order effects, and other multiple sources of associative interference (McGuire, 1961).

Social responses are generally composed of a large number of different behavioral units combined in a particular manner. Responses of higher-order complexity are produced by combinations of previously learned components which may, in themselves, represent relatively complicated behavioral patterns. Consequently, the rate of acquisition of intricate matching responses through observation will be largely determined by the extent to which the necessary components are contained in the observer's repertoire. A person who possesses a very narrow repertoire of behavior, for example, will, in all probability, display only fragmentary imitation of a model's behavior; on the other hand, a person who has acquired most of the relevant components is likely to perform precisely matching responses following several demonstrations. In the case of young preschool children their motor repertoires are more highly developed than their repertoires of verbal responses. It is, perhaps, for this reason that even in the positive-incentive condition, children reproduced a substantially higher percentage (67%) of imitative motor responses than matching verbalizations (20%). A similar pattern of differential imitation was obtained in a previous experiment (Bandura & Huston, 1961) in which preschool children served as subjects.

It is apparent from the foregoing discussion that considerably more research is needed in identifying variables that combine with contiguous stimulation in governing the process of imitative response acquisition.

It is possible, of course, to interpret the present acquisition data as reflecting the operation of generalization from a prior history of reinforcement of imitative behavior. Within any social group, models typically exhibit the accumulated cultural repertoires that have proved most successful for given stimulus situations; consequently, matching the behavior of other persons, particularly the superiors in an age-grade or prestige hierarchy, will maximize positive reinforcement and minimize the frequency of aversive response consequences. Since both the occurrence and the positive reinforcement of matching responses, whether by accident or by intent, are inevitable during the course of social development, no definitive resolution of the reinforcement issue is possible, except through an experiment utilizing organisms that have experienced complete social isolation from birth. It is evident, however, that contemporaneous reinforcements are unnecessary for the acquisition of new matching responses.

The finding that boys perform more imitative aggression than girls as a result of exposure to an aggressive male model, is in accord with results from related experiments (Bandura et al., 1961; 1963a). The additional findings, however, that the introduction of positive incentives practically wiped out the prior performance disparity strongly suggests that the frequently observed sex differences in aggression (Goodenough, 1931; Johnson, 1951; Sears, 1951) may reflect primarily differences in willingness to exhibit aggressive responses, rather than deficits in learning or "masculine-role identification."

The subgroups of children who displayed significant increments in imitative behavior as a function of positive reinforcement were boys who had observed the aggressive model punished, and girls for whom physically aggressive behavior is typically labeled sex inappropriate and nonrewarded or even negatively reinforced. The inhibitory effects of differing reinforcement histories for aggression were clearly reflected in the observation that boys were more easily disinhibited than girls in the reward phase of the experiment. This factor may account for the small sex difference that was obtained even in the positive-incentive condition.

The present study provides further evidence that response inhibition and response disinhibition can be vicariously transmitted through observation of reinforcing consequences to a model's behavior. It is interesting to note, however, that the performance by a model of socially disapproved or prohibited responses (for example, kicking, striking with objects) without the occurrence of any aversive consequences may produce disinhibitory effects analogous to a positive reinforcement operation. These findings are similar to results from studies of direct reinforcement (Crandall, Good, & Crandall, 1964) in which nonreward functioned as a positive reinforcer to increase the probability of the occurrence of formerly punished responses.

Punishment administered to the model apparently further reinforced the girls' existing inhibitions over aggression and produced remarkably little imitative behavior; the boys displayed a similar, though not significant, decrease in imitation. This difference may be partly a function of the relative dominance of aggressive responses in the repertoires of boys and girls. It is also possible that vicarious reinforcement for boys, deriving from the model's successful execution of aggressive behavior (that is, overpowering the noncompliant adversary), may have reduced the effects of externally administered terminal punishment. These factors, as well as the model's self-rewarding and self-punishing reactions following the display of aggression, will be investigated in a subsequent experiment.

R E F E R E N C E S

BAER, D. M., & SHERMAN, J. A. 1964. Reinforcement control of generalized imitation in young children. *Journal of Experimental Child Psychology*, 1, 37–49.

BANDURA, A. 1962. Social learning through imitation. In M. R. Jones (Ed.), *Nebraska symposium on motivation: 1962*. Lincoln: University of Nebraska Press. Pp. 211–269.

BANDURA, A. 1965. Vicarious processes: A case of no-trial learning. In L. Berkowitz (Ed.), *Advances in experimental social psychology*. Vol. 2. New York: Academic Press. Pp. 1–55.

BANDURA, A., & HUSTON, ALETHA C. 1961. Identification as a process of incidental learning. *Journal of Abnormal and Social Psychology*, 63, 311–318.

BANDURA, A., ROSS, DOROTHEA, & ROSS, SHEILA A. 1961. Transmission of aggression through imitation of aggressive models. *Journal of Abnormal and Social Psychology*, 63, 575–582.

BANDURA, A., ROSS, DOROTHEA, & ROSS, SHEILA A. 1963a. Imitation of film-mediated aggressive models. *Journal of Abnormal and Social Psychology*, 66, 3–11.

BANDURA, A., ROSS, DOROTHEA, & ROSS, SHEILA A. 1963b. Vicarious reinforcement and imitative learning. *Journal of Abnormal and Social Psychology*, 67, 601–607.

BANDURA, A., & WALTERS, R. H. 1963. *Social learning and personality development*. New York: Holt, Rinehart, & Winston.

CRANDALL, VIRGINIA C., GOOD, SUZANNE, & CRANDALL, V. J. 1964. The reinforcement effects of adult reactions and non-reactions on children's achievement expectations: A replication study. *Child Development*, 35, 385–397.

GOODENOUGH, FLORENCE L. 1931. *Anger in young children*. Minneapolis: University of Minnesota Press.

JOHNSON, ELIZABETH Z. 1951. Attitudes of children toward authority as projected in their doll play at two age levels. Unpublished doctoral dissertation, Harvard University.

McGUIRE, W. J. 1961. Interpolated motivational statements within a programmed series of instructions as a distribution of practice factor. In A. A. Lumsdaine (Ed.), *Student response in programmed instruction: A symposium.* Washington, D. C.: National Academy of Sciences, National Research Council. Pp. 411–415.

MILLER, N. E., & DOLLARD, J. 1941. *Social learning and imitation.* New Haven: Yale University Press.

MOWRER, O. H. 1960. *Learning theory and the symbolic processes.* New York: Wiley.

SEARS, PAULINE S. 1951. Doll play aggression in normal young children: Influence of sex, age, sibling status, father's absence. *Psychological Monographs,* 65 (6, Whole No. 323).

SHEFFIELD, F. D. 1961. Theoretical considerations in the learning of complex sequential tasks from demonstration and practice. In A. A. Lumsdaine (Ed.), *Student response in programmed instruction: A symposium.* Washington, D. C.: National Academy of Sciences, National Research Council. Pp. 13–32.

SHEFFIELD, F. D., & MACCOBY, N. 1961. Summary and interpretation on research on organizational principles in constructing filmed demonstrations. In A. A. Lumsdaine (Ed.), *Student response in programmed instruction: A symposium.* Washington, D. C.: National Academy of Sciences, National Research Council. Pp. 117–131.

WALTERS, R. H., LEAT, MARION, & MEZEI, L. 1963. Inhibition and disinhibition of responses through empathetic learning. *Canadian Journal of Psychology,* 17, 235–243.

5

The Development of Imitation by Reinforcing Behavioral Similarity to a Model

DONALD M. BAER

ROBERT F. PETERSON

JAMES A. SHERMAN

The development of a class of behaviors which may fairly be called "imitation" is an interesting task, partly because of its relevance to the process of socialization in general and language development in particular, and partly because of its potential value as a training technique for children who require special methods of instruction. Imitation is not a specific set of behaviors that can be exhaustively listed. Any behavior may be considered imitative if it temporally follows behavior demonstrated

* A portion of this research was presented at the biennial meeting of the Society for Research in Child Development, Minneapolis, Minnesota,

by someone else, called a model, and if its topography is functionally controlled by the topography of the model's behavior.
Specifically, this control is such that an observer will note a close
similarity between the topography of the model's behavior and
that of the imitator. Furthermore, this similarity to the model's
behavior will be characteristic of the imitator in responding to a
wide variety of the model's behaviors. Such control could result,
for example, if topographical similarity to a model's behavior
were a reinforcing stimulus dimension for the imitator.

There are, of course, other conditions which can produce similar behaviors from two organisms on the same occasion, or on
similar occasions at different times. One possibility is that both
organisms independently have been taught the same responses to
the same cues; thus, all children recite the multiplication tables
in very similar ways. This similarity does not deserve the label
imitation, and hardly ever receives it; one child's recitation is not
usually a cue to another's, and the similarity of their behavior is
not usually a reinforcer for the children. Nevertheless, the children of this example have similar behaviors.

The fact that the world teaches many children similar lessons
can lead to an arrangement of their behaviors which comes
closer to a useful meaning of imitation. Two children may both
have learned similar responses; one child, however, may respond
at appropriate times whereas the other does not. In that case, the
undiscriminating child may learn to use this response when the
discriminating one does. The term imitation still need not be applied, since the similarity between the two children's responses is
not functional for either of them; in particular, the second child
is not affected by the fact that his behavior is similar to that of

March, 1965. This research was supported by PHS grant MH-02208,
National Institute of Mental Health, entitled An Experimental Analysis
of Social Motivation. Mr. Frank Junkin, Superintendent, Dr. Ralph
Hayden, Medical Director, and other members of the staff of the Fircrest
School, Seattle, Washington, made space and subjects available. We
wish to thank Mrs. Joan Beavers for her help as a "new" experimenter
in the tests of generalization and for assistance in the preparation of this
manuscript.

the first. This arrangement approaches one which Miller and Dollard (1941) call "matched-dependent" behavior. One organism responds to the behavior of another merely as a discriminative stimulus with respect to the timing of his own behavior; many times, these behaviors will happen to be alike, because both organisms will typically use the most efficient response, given enough experience.

It should be possible, however, to arrange the behavior of two organisms so that one of them will, in a variety of ways, produce precise topographical similarity to the other, but nothing else. A study by Baer and Sherman (1964) seemingly showed the result of such prior learning in several young children. In that study, reinforcements were arranged for children's imitations of three activities of an animated, talking puppet, which served both as a model and a source of social reinforcement for imitating. As a result of this reinforcement, a fourth response of the puppet was spontaneously imitated by the children, although that imitation had never before been reinforced. When reinforcement of the other three imitations was discontinued, the fourth, never-reinforced imitation also decreased in strength; when reinforcement of the original imitations was resumed, imitation of the fourth response again rose in rate, although it still was never reinforced. In short, these children apparently generalized along a stimulus dimension of similarity between their behaviors and the behaviors of a model: when similarity to the model in three different ways was reinforced, they thereupon displayed a fourth way of achieving similarity to the model. Thus, similarity between their behavior and the model's was a functional stimulus in their behavior.

Metz (1965) demonstrated the development of some imitative behavior in two autistic children who initially showed little or no imitative response. In this study, responses similar in topography to demonstrations by the experimenter were reinforced with "Good" and food. Metz found that, after intensive training, several imitative responses could be maintained in strength even when not reinforced with food, and that the subjects had a higher probability of imitating new responses after training than before. However, in one of the conditions used to evaluate the subjects' imitative repertoire before and after imitative training, "Good" was still said contingent upon correct new imitations. Thus, for one subject who initially showed a non-zero rate of imitation, it could be argued that the increased imitation in the test after training was due to an experimentally developed reinforcing property of "Good," rather than to the imitation training as such. Further, in the Metz study, due to a lack of extinction or other manipulation of the behavior, it is difficult to specify that the higher probability of imitating new responses, and the maintenance of unreinforced imitative responses, were in fact due to the reinforcement of the initial imitative responses during training.

Lovaas, Berberich, Perloff, and Schaeffer (1966) used shaping and fading procedures to establish imitative speech in two autistic children. They reported that as training progressed and more vocal behavior came under the control of a model's prior vocalization, it became progressively easier to obtain new imitative vocalizations. When reinforcement was shifted from an imitative-contingent schedule to a basically non-contingent schedule, imitative behavior deteriorated. In an additional manipulation, the model presented Norwegian words interspersed with English words for the children to imitate. Initially, the children did not reproduce the Norwegian words perfectly. However, the authors judged that the subjects gradually improved their imitations of the Norwegian words even though these imitations were not reinforced.

The studies by Baer and Sherman (1964), Metz (1965), Lovaas et al. (1966), and other reports (Bandura, 1962) suggest that for children with truly imitative repertoires, induction has occurred, such that (1) relatively novel behaviors can be developed before direct shaping, merely by providing an appropriate demonstration by a model, and (2) some imitative responses can be maintained, although unreinforced, as long as other imitative responses are reinforced.

The purpose of the present study was to extend the generality of the above findings and to demonstrate a method of producing a truly imitative repertoire in children initially lacking one.

METHOD

Subjects

Three children, 9 to 12 years of age, were selected from several groups of severely and profoundly retarded children in a state school. They were chosen not because they were retarded, but because they seemed to be the only children available of a practical age who apparently showed no imitation whatsoever. (The success of the method to be described suggests that it may have considerable practical value for the training of such children.) The subjects were without language, but made occasional grunting vocalizations, and responded to a few simple verbal commands ("Come here," "Sit down," etc.). They were ambulatory (but typically had developed walking behavior relatively late in their development, in the sixth or seventh year), could dress themselves, were reasonably well toilet trained, and could feed themselves. Fair eye-hand coordination was evident, and simple manipulatory skills were present.

The subjects were chosen from groups of children initially observed in their wards from a distance over a period of several days. No instances of possible imitation were noted in the subjects finally selected. (That is, on no occasion did any subject display behavior similar to that of another person, except in instances where a common stimulus appeared to be controlling the behaviors of both persons, for example, both going to the dining area when food was displayed on the table.) Subsequently, an experimenter approached and engaged the subjects in extended play. In the course of this play, he would repeatedly ask them to imitate some simple response that he demonstrated, such as clapping his hands, or waving. The children failed to imitate any of these responses, although they clearly were capable of at least some of them. Finally, during the training itself, every sample of behavior was initially presented to the child as a demonstration accompanied by the command, "Do this"; at first, none of these samples was imitated, despite extensive repetition.

First Training Procedures

Each subject was seen at mealtimes, once or twice a day, three to five times a week. The subject's food was used as a reinforcer. It was delivered a spoonful at a time by the experimenter, who always said "Good" just before putting the spoon into the subject's mouth. The subject and experimenter faced each other across the corner of a small table, on which were placed the food tray and the experimenter's records. Elsewhere in the room was another small table on which were placed some materials used later in the study, a desk with a telephone on it, a coat rack holding one or more coats, a wastebasket, and a few other chairs.

The basic procedure was to teach each subject a series of discriminated operants. Each discriminated operant consisted of three elements: a discriminative stimulus (S^d) presented by the experimenter, a correct response by the subject, and reinforcement after a correct response. The S^d was the experimenter's command, "Do this", followed by his demonstration of some behavior. The response required was one similar to the experimenter's. Thus, the operant learned was always topographically imitative of the experimenter's demonstration. The reinforcement was food, preceded by the word "Good".

Since none of the subjects was imitative, none of the initial S^d's was followed by any behavior which resembled that demonstrated by the experimenter. This was true even for those behaviors which the subjects were clearly capable of performing. Subject 1, for example, would sit down when told to, but did not imitate the experimenter when he said "Do this", sat down, and then offered her the chair. Hence, the initial imitative training for all subjects was accomplished with a combination of shaping

(Skinner, 1953) and fading (Terrace, 1963a, 1963b) or "putting through" procedures (Konorski and Miller, 1937).

The first response of the program for Subject 1 was to raise an arm after the experimenter had raised his. The subject was presented with a series of arm-raising demonstrations by the experimenter, each accompanied by "Do this," to which she made no response. The experimenter than repeated the demonstration, reached out, took the subject's hand and raised it for her, and then immediately reinforced her response. After several trials of this sort, the experimenter began gradually to fade out his assistance by raising the subject's arm only part way and shaping the completion of the response. Gradually, the experimenter's assistance was faded until the subject made an unassisted arm-raising response whenever the experimenter raised his arm. The initial responses for all subjects were taught in this manner whenever necessary.

Occasionally during the very early training periods a subject would resist being guided through a response. For example, with a response involving arm raising, Subject 3 at first pulled his arm downward whenever the experimenter attempted to raise it. In this case, the experimenter merely waited and tried again until the arm could be at least partially raised without great resistance; then the response was reinforced. After subjects had received a few reinforcements following the experimenter's assistance in performing a response, they no longer resisted. As the number of responses in the subjects' repertoire increased, the experimenter discontinued the guiding procedure and relied only on shaping procedures when a response did not match the demonstration.

A number of responses, each topographically similar to a demonstration by the experimenter, was taught to each subject. Training of most responses was continued until its demonstration was reliably matched by the subject. The purpose of these initial training procedures was to program reinforcement, in as many and diverse ways as practical, whenever a subject's behavior was topographically similar to that demonstrated by the experimenter.

Further Training Procedures

PROBES FOR IMITATION

As the initial training procedures progressed, and the subjects began to come under the control of the experimenter's demonstrations, certain responses were demonstrated which, if imitated perfectly on their first presentation, were deliberately not reinforced on the first or any future occasion. These responses served as probes for the developing imitative nature of the subject's repertoire. A list of the responses demonstrated, including the reinforced ones for the initial training procedure and the unreinforced probe demonstrations, is given in Table 5.1 for Subject 1. These responses are listed in the order of first demonstration. Subject 1 had 95 reinforced and 35 unreinforced responses. Similar responses were used with Subjects 2 and 3. Subject 2 had 125 reinforced and five unreinforced probes; Subject 3 had eight reinforced responses and one unreinforced probe.

During the probes, the experimenter continued to present S^d's for imitation. If the response demonstrated belonged to the group of reinforced responses and the subject imitated within 10 seconds, reinforcement ("Good" and food) was delivered and the next response was demonstrated. If the subject did not imitate within 10 seconds, no reinforcement was delivered and the experimenter demonstrated the next response. If it belonged to the unreinforced group of responses (probes), and if the subject imitated it, there were no programmed consequences and the experimenter demonstrated the next response no sooner than 10 seconds after the subject's imitation. If it was not imitated, the experimenter performed the next demonstration 10 seconds later. The purpose of the 10-second delay was to minimize the possibility that the subjects' unreinforced imitations were being maintained by the possible reinforcing effects of the presentation of an S^d for a to-be-reinforced imitative response. Demonstrations for reinforced and unreinforced responses were presented to subjects in any unsystematic order.

TABLE 5.1: *The Sequence of Responses Demonstrated to Subject 1. Asterisks indicate unreinforced responses.*

1. Raise left arm.
2. Tap table with left hand
3. Tap chest with left hand
4. Tap head with left hand
5. Tap left knee with left hand
6. Tap right knee with left hand
7. Tap nose
*8. Tap arm of chair
9. Tap leg of table
10. Tap leg with left hand
11. Extend left arm
*12. Make circular motion with arm
13. Stand up
14. Both hands on ears
15. Flex arm
16. Nod yes
17. Tap chair seat
18. Extend both arms
19. Put feet on chair
20. Walk around
21. Make vocal response
22. Extend right arm sideways
23. Tap shoulder
24. Tap head with right hand
25. Tap right knee with right hand
26. Tap leg with right hand
27. Tap left knee with right hand
28. Raise right arm overhead
29. Tap chest with right hand
30. Tap table with right hand
31. Move chair
32. Sit in chair
33. Throw paper in basket
34. Pull up socks
35. Tap desk
36. Climb on chair
37. Open door
38. Move ash tray
39. Put paper in chair
40. Sit in two chairs (chained)
41. Tap chair with right hand
42. Move paper from basket to desk
43. Move box from shelf to desk
44. Put on hat
45. Move hat from table to desk
46. Move box from shelf to desk
47. Nest three boxes
48. Put hat in chair
49. Tap wall
50. Move waste basket
51. Move paper from desk to table
52. Stand in corner
53. Pull window shade
54. Place box in chair
55. Walk around desk
56. Smile
57. Protrude tongue
58. Put head on desk
*59. Ring bell
60. Nest two boxes
61. Crawl on floor
*62. Walk with arms above head
63. Sit on floor
64. Put arm behind back (standing)
65. Walk with right arm held up
66. Throw box
*67. Walk to telephone
*68. Extend both arms (sitting)

69. Walk and tap head with left hand
70. Walk and tap head with right hand
*71. Walk and clap hands
*72. Open mouth
73. Jump
74. Pat radiator
*75. Nod no
76. Pick up phone
77. Pull drawer
78. Pet coat
79. Tear kleenex
80. Nest four boxes
81. Point gun and say "Bang"
*82. Put towel over face
*83. Put hands over eyes
*84. Tap floor
*85. Scribble
*86. Move toy car on table
87. Place circle in form board
88. Place circle, square, and triangle in form board
*89. Crawl under table
*90. Walk and clap sides
*91. Lie on floor
*92. Kick box
*93. Put foot over table rung
*94. Fly airplane
*95. Rock doll
*96. Burp doll
*97. Tap chair with bat
*98. Open and close book
99. Work egg beater
100. Put arm through hoop
101. Build three block tower
*102. Stab self with rubber knife
103. Put blocks in ring
104. Walk and hold book on head
105. Ride kiddie car
106. Sweep with broom
107. Place beads around neck
108. Ride hobby horse
*109. Put on glove
110. Use whisk broom on table
111. Work rolling pin
*112. Push large car
113. Put beads on doorknob
*114. Put hat on hobby horse
115. Sweep block with broom
116. Place box inside ring of beads
117. Put glove in pocket of lab coat
118. Push button on tape recorder
*119. Bang spoon on desk
120. Lift cup
121. Use whisk broom on a wall
*122. Put a cube in a cup
123. Rattle a spoon in a cup
*124. Throw paper on the floor
*125. Hug a pillow
126. Tap pegs into pegboard with hammer
*127. Wave a piece of paper
*128. Shake a rattle
*129. Hit two spoons together
130. Shake a tambourine

NON-REINFORCEMENT OF ALL IMITATION

After the probe phase, and after stable performances of reinforced and unreinforced imitative responses were established, non-reinforcement of all imitative behavior was programmed. The purpose of this procedure was to show the dependence of the imitative repertoire on the food reinforcement which was apparently responsible for its development.

Non-reinforcement of imitation was instituted in the form of reinforcement for any behavior other than imitation. Differential reinforcement of other behavior is abbreviated DRO (Reynolds, 1961). The experimenter continued saying "Good" and feeding the subject, but not contingent on imitations. Instead, the experimenter delivered reinforcement at least 20 seconds after the subject's last imitation had taken place. Thus, for the group of previously reinforced responses, the only change between reinforcement and non-reinforcement periods was a shift in the contingency. For the group of unreinforced or probe responses there was no change; food reforcement still did not follow either the occurrence or non-occurrence of an imitative response. This procedure involved simultaneously the extinction of imitation and also the reinforcement of whatever other responses may have been taking place at the moment of reinforcement.

For Subject 1, the DRO period was 30 seconds. For Subject 2, DRO periods were 30, 60, and 0 seconds. (DRO 0-second meant reinforcement was delivered immediately after the S^d, before an imitative response could occur.) This sequence of DRO intervals was used because, as displayed in the Results section, Subject 2 maintained stable imitation under the initial DRO procedures, unlike the other subjects. For Subject 3, the DRO period was 20 seconds. After the DRO procedure for each subject, contingent reinforcement of imitation was resumed and the procedures described below were instituted.

IMITATIVE CHAINS

After reinforcement for imitative behavior was resumed with Subjects 1 and 2, the procedure of chaining together old and new imitations was begun. At first only two-response chains were demonstrated; then three-response chains, after two-response chains were successfully achieved; and so on. During chaining, the experimenter demonstrated the responses the subject was to imitate as an unbroken series. In all cases, the demonstrated chain contained both responses previously learned by the subject and relatively new ones. Walking from one locale to another in the process of performing these behaviors was not considered part of the imitative chain and was not judged for imitative accuracy.

VERBAL IMITATIONS

Late in the training program for Subjects 1 and 3, when virtually any new motor performance by the experimenter was almost certain to be imitated, vocal performances were begun with simple sounds. The experimenter, as usual, said "Do this," but instead of making some motor response made a vocal one, for example, "Ah." Subjects 1 and 3 repeatedly failed to imitate such demonstrations. Different procedures were then employed to obtain vocal imitations. For Subject 1, the vocal response to be imitated was set into a chain of non-vocal responses. For example, the experimenter would say, "Do this," rise from his chair and walk to the center of the room, turn towards the subject, say "Ah," and return to his seat. To such a demonstration Subject 1 responded by leaving her seat, walking toward the center of the room, turning toward the experimenter, and then beginning a series of facial and vocal responses out of which eventually emerged an "Ah" sufficiently similar to the experimenter's to merit reinforcement. This coupling of motor and vocal performances was maintained for several more demonstrations, during which the motor performance was made successively shorter and more economical of motion; finally, the experimenter was able to remain seated, say "Do this," say "Ah," and immediately evoke an imitation from the subject. Proceeding in this manner, simple sounds were shaped and then combined into longer or more complex sounds and finally into usable words.

Subject 3, like Subject 1, initially failed to imitate vocalizations. In his case, the experimenter proceeded to demonstrate a set of motor performances which moved successively closer to vocalizations. At first the experimenter obtained imitative blowing out of a lighted match, then blowing without the match, then more vigorous blowing which included an initial plosive "p", then added a voiced component to the blowing which was shaped into a "Pah" sound. Proceeding in this manner, a number of vocalizations were produced, all as reliable imitations.

GENERALIZATION TO OTHER EXPERIMENTERS

When the imitative repertoire of Subject 1 had developed to a high level, new experimenters were presented to her, of the opposite or the same sex as the original male experimenter. These novel experimenters gave the same demonstrations as the original experimenter in the immediately preceding session. The purpose of this procedure was to investigate whether the subject's imitative repertoire was limited to demonstrations by the original male experimenter. During this procedure, the new experimenters delivered reinforcement in the same manner as the original experimenter; for example, previously reinforced imitations were reinforced and probes were not.

RESULTS

Reliability of Scoring Imitative Responses

Checks on the reliability of the experimenter's scoring of any response as imitative were made at scattered points throughout the study for Subjects 1 and 2. The percentage of agreement between the experimenter's scoring and the independent records of a second observer exceeded 98%.

First Training Procedures

The initial training procedure contained occasions when the extent of the developing imitative repertoire of each subject could be seen. These were occasions when behavior was demonstrated by the experimenter to the subject for the first time. Any attempt by the subject to imitate such new behavior before direct

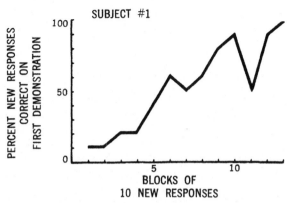

FIGURE 5.1.   The development of imitation in Subject 1

training or shaping could be attributed to the history of reinforcement for matching other behavior of the experimenter.
Thus, it was possible to examine the sequence of initial presentations to each subject to discover any increasing probability that
new behavior would be imitated on its first presentation.

The sequence of 130 responses in Subject 1's program was
sufficient to increase her probability of imitating new responses
from zero at the beginning of the program to 100% at the end.
This was demonstrated by grouping the 130 responses into 13
successive blocks of 10 each. As shown in Figure 5.1, the proportion imitated on the first presentation within each block rose,
not too steadily, but nonetheless clearly, to 100% by the 13th
block.

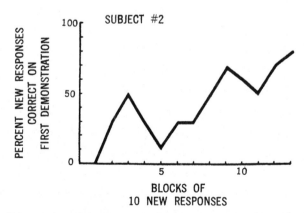

FIGURE 5.2.   The development of imitation in Subject 2

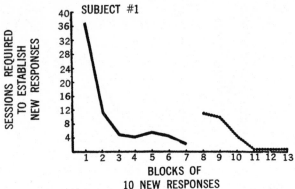

FIGURE 5.3. The rate of development of imitation in Subject 1

The proportion of new responses successfully imitated by Subject 2 upon their first presentation rose from 0% to 80%, through a sequence of 130 new responses, as shown in Figure 5.2.

Subject 2 displayed both more variable and less thorough imitation of new responses on their first presentation than did Subject 1, although the general form of the data is similar.

Subject 3 was taught only eight discriminated operants of imitative topography, which he acquired much more rapidly than did either Subject 1 or 2. He imitated the ninth spontaneously on its first presentation, although he had not imitated it before training.

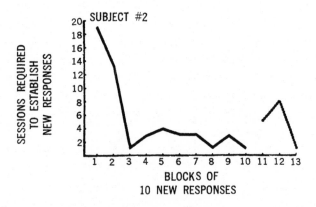

FIGURE 5.4. The rate of development of imitation in Subject 2

The progressive development of imitation was apparent in other aspects of the data as well. The number of training sessions required to establish new imitations was displayed by plotting this number of sessions for each successive block of 10 new responses. The criterion for establishment of a new imitative response was that, for one trial, a subject displayed the response demonstrated by the experimenter with no shaping or fading procedures required for that trial. This is shown in Figure 5.3 for Subject 1 and in Figure 5.4 for Subject 2, as solid lines. Both graphs show a systematically decreasing number of sessions required to establish successive new imitations. The dotted portions of each graph represent deviations from the usual types of training procedure and thus are plotted differently. For Subject 1 the dotted portion represents a period in which verbal responses were introduced (not plotted as part of Figure 5.3, but discussed later in this report). For Subject 2 the dotted portion represents a sequence of sessions in which few new imitative re-

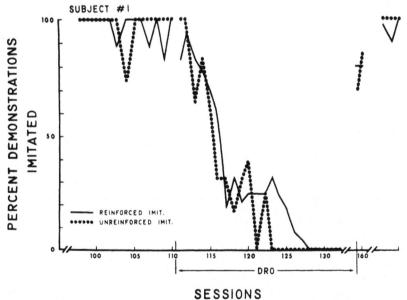

FIGURE 5.5.   The maintenance and extinction of reinforced and unreinforced imitation in Subject 1 (The breaks in the data before and after session 160 represent periods of experimentation aimed at other problems.)

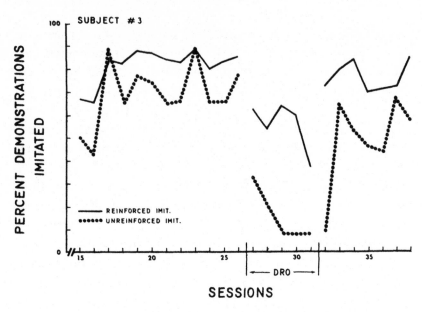

FIGURE 5.6. The maintenance and extinction of reinforced and unreinforced imitation in Subject 3

sponses were introduced. Rather, two previously established imitative responses of similar topography, which the subject no longer clearly displayed, were worked on intensively.

DRO Procedures

For all subjects, both reinforced and unreinforced imitative behavior was maintained over continuing experimental sessions as long as food reinforcement was contingent upon at least some imitative behavior. When reinforcement was no longer contingent upon imitative behavior during the DRO periods, both the previously reinforced imitations and the never-reinforced probe imitations decreased markedly in strength.

Figure 5.5 is a plot of the percentages of each type of imitative response by Subject 1. It shows that her probability of imitating the 35 probes varied between 80 and 100%, as long as the other 95 imitations, within which the probes were interspersed, were reinforced. The application of the DRO 30-second procedure extinguished virtually all imitative behavior within about 20 hours. The previously reinforced imitations and the probe imitations extinguished alike in rate and degree. All imitative behavior recovered when, with a small amount of shaping, reinforcement was again made contingent upon imitative behavior.

Figure 5.6 is a similar plot of the imitative behavior of Subject 3. It shows the maintenance of the one probe imitation and eight reinforced imitations during reinforcement of imitation, a marked decrease in both types of imitative behavior during the DRO 20-second period, and a recovery when contingent reinforcement of imitations was resumed.

Figure 5.7 is a plot of the imitative behavior of Subject 2. Her results were similar to those obtained for Subjects 1 and 3, in terms of the maintenance of 125 reinforced and five probe imitations, under conditions of reinforcement of imitations. However, her data depart from the others' during the DRO period. Initially, this subject showed no reliable signs of extinction after

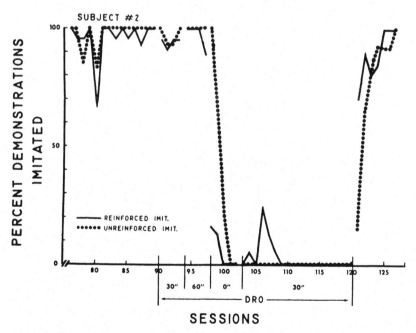

FIGURE 5.7.   The maintenance and extinction of reinforced and unreinforced imitation in Subject 2

four sessions of DRO with a 30-second delay. Next, DRO 60-second was instituted for four sessions, still without any reliable effect. At that point, a procedure of DRO 0-second was begun, meaning that the experimenter demonstrated some behavior, and instantly, before the subject could respond, said "Good" and delivered the food to her mouth. Thus, reinforcement served to forestall the durable imitative responses this subject was displaying. Figure 5.7 demonstrates the immediacy of effect of this procedure. After four sessions of DRO 0-second, it was possible to resume the procedures of DRO 30-seconds and produce only a brief and partial recovery of the rate of imitation, which then declined to zero. A return to contingent reinforcement, with a small amount of shaping, quickly reinstated the high rate of imitation previously displayed.

In all cases, then, it is clear that the imitative repertoire depended on reinforcement of at least some of its members. It is noteworthy that those responses which had developed and been maintained previously without direct reinforcement could not survive extinction applied to the entire class of behaviors.

Imitative Chains

Subjects 1 and 2 were exposed to the procedure of chaining together old and new imitative responses. At the end of 10 hours of the procedure for Subject 1, lengthy chains containing already established and new imitative responses became practical. It was possible to obtain perfect imitation on 90% of the chains, some of which involved as many as five responses. Subject 2 received only 2 hours of training on chains. At the end of this time, she would imitate 50% of the three-response chains demonstrated to her, and 80% of the two-response chains.

Verbal Behavior

Subjects 1 and 3 were used in the procedures for the development of verbal imitation. Verbal imitations were established for Subject 1 by chaining together motor and vocal behaviors and then fading out the motor components. Twenty hours of training resulted in 10 words which were reliably imitated such as, "Hi," "Okay," the subject's name, and the names of some objects. Subject 3's training in vocal imitations was accomplished by evoking a set of motor imitations which moved successively closer to vocalizations. Approximately 10 hours of training produced the reliable imitative vocalizations of seven vowel and consonant sounds.

Generalization to Other Experimenters

When Subject 1 was presented with new experimenters, of both the opposite and same sex as the original male experimenter, she showed approximately the same degree of imitation displayed to the original experimenter. That is, she imitated all of the three probe demonstrations given by one new male experimenter and imitated 12 of 15 reinforced demonstrations by a second new male experimenter on the first demonstration and the remaining three by the third demonstration. On another occasion, the second new male experimenter re-presented the 15 demonstrations; all were imitated on their first demonstration. The subject also imitated all of a series of demonstrations by a female experimenter.

DISCUSSION

The procedures of this study were sufficient to produce highly developed imitation in the experimental subjects. However a noteworthy point is the relative difficulty experienced in obtaining initial matching responses from a subject even when the response required (for example, arm raising) clearly was in the subject's current repertoire. This suggests that the subjects were not so much learning specific responses as learning the instruction, "Do as the experimenter does." Initially, then, the procedures of this study seem to have involved bringing a number of the subjects' responses under the instructional control of the experimenter's demonstration.* To establish this type of instructional control by demonstration requires that the subjects either have or develop responses of observing their own behavior as well as the experimenter's behavior.

As an increasing number of the subjects' behaviors came under the instructional control of demonstration, additional behavior, not previously observed in the subjects' repertoires, became increasingly probable, merely as a result of presenting an appropriate demonstration by a model. In the terminology suggested by Miller and Dollard (1941), a sufficiently extensive arrangement of one child's behavior into matched-dependent response with a model's behavior was sufficient to induce a tendency to achieve similarity in more ways than were originally taught.

The development of imitative repertoires, including the unreinforced imitation of probe demonstrations, could be accounted for by the effects of conditioned reinforcement. Conditioned reinforcement may have operated in the present study in the following way: the basic procedure was that of teaching the subject a series of responses, each of which was topographically similar to a demonstration just given by a model. Initially, each response had to be established separately. When established, such responses were imitative only topographically and would better be called matched-dependent behavior; the fact that a subject's response was similar to the experimenter's behavior at that point had no functional significance for any of the subject's other responses. Nevertheless, topographical similarity between child and experimenter was there to be attended to by the child, and this similarity was potentially discriminative with respect to the only reinforcement delivered in the experimental situation. One of the most effective ways of giving a stimulus a reinforcing function is to make it discriminative with respect to reinforcement. In these applications, the stimulus class of behavioral similarity was, in numerous examples, made discriminative with respect to positive reinforcement. Hence, similarity could be

---

* The authors are indebted to Israel Goldiamond for his suggestions in clarifying this point.

expected to take on a positive reinforcing function as well as a discriminative function. As a positive reinforcer, it should strengthen any new behavior that produced or achieved it. Behaviors that achieve similarity between one's self and a model are, of course, imitative behaviors; furthermore, they are imitative by function and not by coincidence.

This analysis is simple only at first inspection. In particular, it should be noted that "similarity" is not a simple stimulus dimension, like the frequency of sound or the intensity of light. Similarity must mean a correspondence of some sort between the stimulus output of the child's behavior and the stimulus output of the model's. A correspondence between two stimuli is not too esoteric a stimulus to consider as functional in controlling behavior. However, for an imitative repertoire to develop, a class of correspondences must become functional as stimuli. The child must learn to discriminate a correspondence between the appearance of his hand and the model's hand, his arm and the model's arm, his leg and the model's leg, his voice and the model's voice, etc. It would seem reasonable that each of these kinds of difference must require some prior experience on the child's part to appreciate. A scantiness of such experience may well be characteristic of retarded children, and makes them intriguing subjects for such studies. The ability to generalize similarities among a considerable variety of stimuli, which the children of these studies evidenced, suggests that the training they were subjected to was adequate to the problem. An immediate next problem, it would seem, is the detailed analysis of those procedures to find out which of them accomplished what part of this generalization. That analysis might yield a fair understanding of imitative behavior.

REFERENCES

BAER, D. M., & SHERMAN, J. A. 1964. Reinforcement control of generalized imitation in young children. *Journal of Experimental Child Psychology*, 1, 37–49.

150 : *The Development of Imitation*

BANDURA, A. 1962. Social learning through imitation. In M. R. Jones (Ed.), *Nebraska symposium on motivation*. Lincoln: University of Nebraska Press. Pp. 211–269.

KONORSKI, J., & MILLER, S. 1937. On two types of conditioned reflex. *Journal of General Psychology*, 16, 264–272.

LOVAAS, O. I., BERBERICH, J. P., PERLOFF, B. F., & SCHAEFFER, B. 1966. Acquisition of imitative speech by schizophrenic children. *Science*, 151, 705–707.

METZ, J. R. 1965. Conditioning generalized imitation in autistic children. *Journal of Experimental Child Psychology*, 2, 389–399.

MILLER, N. E., & DOLLARD, J. 1941, *Social learning and imitation*. New Haven: Yale University Press.

REYNOLDS, G. S. 1961. Behavioral contrast. *Journal of Experimental Analysis of Behavior*, 4, 57–71.

SKINNER, B. F. 1953. *Science and human behavior*. New York: Macmillan.

TERRACE, H. S. 1963a. Discrimination learning with and without "errors". *Journal of Experimental Analysis of Behavior*, 6, 1–27.

TERRACE, H. S. 1963b. Errorless transfer of a discrimination across two continua. *Journal of Experimental Analysis of Behavior*, 6, 223–232.

6 Influence of Response Consequences to a Social Model on Resistance to Deviation

RICHARD H. WALTERS
ROSS D. PARKE

Social control is to a large extent maintained through vicariously experienced reward and punishment. Adverse consequences to deviant members of society and the social rewards that accrue to those who perform socially approved acts are widely publicized through the mass media and the pronouncements of representatives of social institutions. In a paral-

Reprinted by permission of the publisher and author from the JOURNAL OF EXPERIMENTAL CHILD PSYCHOLOGY, 1964, Vol. 1, pp. 269–280.

The authors wish to express their appreciation to the Superintendents of Public Schools of York Township and Kitchener and to the Director of Recreation, Kitchener, for their cooperation in this study; and to Valerie Cane, Patsie Hutton, and David Walters for assistance in collecting the data. Thanks are due to Arthur Jenoff, Marjorie Stewart, and Eric Wilson for assistance in making the films. The study was supported by the Public Health Research Grant 605-5-293 of the (Canadian) National Health Grants Program and the Defence Research Board of Canada Grant 9401-24.

lel fashion, parents and other socialization agents utilize the story with a moral as a means of teaching their children to conform to social demands and to resist deviation.

In spite of the implicit recognition by agents of social control of the possible inhibitory and disinhibitory effects of models, these effects have only recently been emphasized in theoretical discussions of imitative behavior (Bandura & Walters, 1963; Hill, 1960; Mowrer, 1960b). This emphasis has been accompanied by empirical investigations, which have confirmed the popular belief that deviant behavior may be inhibited by the observation of adverse consequences to the model whereas the witnessing of rewarding consequences for deviant behavior may increase the probability that the observer will likewise deviate (Bandura, Ross, & Ross, 1963; Walters, Leat, & Mezei, 1963).

Is it unlikely, however, that direct observation or knowledge of rewards and punishment experienced by social models is a necessary condition for the occurrence of inhibitory or disinhibitory effects. Lefkowitz, Blake, and Mouton (1955) demonstrated greater imitative violation of a prohibition when the model was attired as a high-status person than when the status of the model was apparently low. Since the deviant behavior of high-status individuals is less likely to meet with adverse consequences than that of persons with fewer social advantages, this finding probably indicates that *inferred* consequences to models influences the behavior of observers.

Disinhibition may also occur if an observer sees a model, whatever his status, perform a socially disapproved act with no adverse consequence to himself. For example, adolescents and adults who observed a knife-fight sequence from the film, *Rebel Without a Cause*, showed an increase in physical aggression even though the film sequence was cut at a point at which the outcome of the consequences to the protagonists was doubtful (Walters & Llewellyn Thomas, 1963). No outcome, or "nonreward," in such cases appears to operate similarly to a positive reinforcer and may be conceptualized as withdrawal of punishment rather than as simple nonreward. Of course, the model may not in fact have been punished for the socially disapproved response; it is nevertheless reasonable to believe that this kind of disinhibitory effect occurs only if the response is one for which the observer originally anticipated that adverse consequences would follow.

Walters et al. (1963) compared the responses of three groups of children who were exposed to a "temptation" situation. Prior to this exposure, two groups of children saw a film depicting a small child play with toys that they, the observers, had been forbidden to touch. One of these groups saw the model punished for his deviation, while the other group observed the model rewarded. In comparison to a group of children who saw no film, the reward-movie group showed weaker resistance to deviation. This paper reports a study similar to that carried out by Walters et al. The major extension consisted of the addition of a fourth group of children who saw the model play with forbidden toys with no evident consequence, either rewarding or punishing, resulting from his behavior. It was predicted that the *absence of punishing consequences* would under these circumstances operate similarly to vicariously experienced reward to increase the probability of imitative deviation.

The observation of punishing consequences to a model may have only a temporary effect on behavior. Once a prohibition has been removed, an observer may imitate previously observed responses of the model as much as if he had seen these rewarded or go unpunished. Bandura et al. (1963) found that children who had seen an aggressive model punished showed relatively little imitation in a postexposure test but were nevertheless able to describe the aggressive acts of the model with a great deal of accuracy. The authors interpret their findings as indicating that imitative responses are *learned* on the basis of contiguous association of sensory events (classical conditioning) and that vicariously experienced reinforcements are determinants only of *performance*. As an incidental test of this proposition, all children in the present study were twice observed in the presence of the prohibited toys; first, while the prohibition was still in force (though, in the case of the film groups, after exposure to the model), and during a subsequent period when the prohibition had been removed.

METHOD

Subjects (Ss)

Eighty-four boys, with a mean age of 5 years, 11 months served as Ss. The boys were randomly assigned to one of four groups. Three groups were shown a 3-minute colored film sequence in which the players were a 6-year-old boy and his mother. Three film sequences were used: in one the boy was "rewarded" for playing with some toys, in the second he was "punished" for doing so, while in the third the boy was neither rewarded nor punished. The fourth group saw no movie.

Equipment

The films were prepared by a professional television producer and director. Except for the addition of "endings" to two of the films, the sequences displayed to Ss were identical. Complete correspondence was ensured through the use of copies of an edited sequence. The film showed an adult female, presumably a mother, indicate to a child that he should not play with toys that had been set on a nearby table. The adult then sat the child in a chair beside the table, gave him a book to read, and left the room. After her departure, the child put the book aside and proceeded to play the prohibited toys. Play continued for approximately 2 minutes. The play sequence consisted of "clips" from more lengthy "shots" of the child's play with each of the available toys. The clips were selected in such a way that all the toys were adequately displayed and seven well-defined manipulations of certain toys were included, for example, the child's holding a sparkler close to his face while shooting sparks. A list of these well-defined and clearly identifiable responses was made.

Endings were added to two of the films. In the reward-movie ending, the adult returned to the room, sat beside the child, handed him toys, and played with him affectionately. In the punishment-movie ending, the mother, on returning to the room, snatched from the child the toy with which he was then playing, shook him, and once again set him down in the chair with the book. In the no-consequences film the mother did not reenter the scene.

The services of a professional director ensured that the significance of the mother's behavior was beyond doubt, in spite of the fact that the films were silent. Because children are used to seeing sound-accompanied movies in school settings, a tape recording of background music was played during the showing of the films. The recording was identical for all children.

A portable one-way vision booth, which permitted children to be observed unobtrusively, was erected in the testing room. The booth has been described in more detail by Walters and Demkow (1963); a diagram of furniture arrangements similar to those used in the present study is provided by Walters et al. (1963). On the table in front of the booth, three rows of toys, three toys in each row, were displayed. The S was seated in a chair at one end of the table in front of the toys in the first row, which were thus readily accessible to him. The toys in the second row were accessible if the child stood up in front of the chair, while the third row could be reached only if the child walked around the table.

A Bolex 18-5 projector, which was placed on a table immediately behind the child's chair, was used to project the films on to a screen set against the opposite wall of the room.

Procedure

NO FILM-GROUP

A female E brought the child into the room and said, "You sit here (indicating the chair). Now, these toys have been arranged for someone else, so you'd better not touch them. In a little while I am going to play a game with you, but I have forgotten something and must go and get it. While I'm gone, you can look at this book. (*E* at this point handed *S* a dictionary.) I'm going to close the door so that nobody will bother you; and when I come back, I'll knock, so you'll know it's me."

The child was left alone for 15 minutes. On returning, *E* said, "I still haven't been able to find what I was looking for, but I was talking to the boy that these toys were arranged for, and he said it was OK if you played with them. So you can get out of your seat and play with any of the toys, and I'll be back in a few minutes." *E* then left the room for a further 5 minutes. On returning for a second time, *E* said, "I'm afraid we haven't got time to play the game after all, but I hope you had fun playing with the toys anyway."

FILM GROUPS

E told the boys on the way to the experimental room that they would see a movie. The rest of the procedure was precisely the same as for the no-film group, except that, immediately after telling the child not to touch the toys, *E* said, "Now I'm going to show you a movie." On the completion of the film, *E* continued with the instructions given above, beginning at "In a little while. . . ." As with the no-film group, *E* left the room twice, once for 15 minutes and subsequently for a further 5 minutes.

Measures

An observer who was placed behind the one-way vision booth recorded on a specially prepared record sheet the times at which *S* touched and ceased to touch individual toys. The sheet was set up in such a way that, during the 15-minute period of *E*'s first absence from the room, the observer's only task was to record times, read from a Heuer Century stopwatch, in the appropriate squares which designated specific toys. Prior experience had indicated that perfect interrater reliability could be achieved through this method of data collection (Walters et al., 1963); consequently, only one observer was employed.

From the observer's records, the following scores were calculated: the latency of *S*'s first deviant response, the number of times he deviated, and the total time for which he deviated. In addition, weighted deviation scores were calculated in the following manner: a deviation involving one of the three most accessible toys was scored 1; a deviation involving one of the toys in the second row was scored 2; while *S*'s touching a toy in the third row was scored 3. A weighted number of deviations and a weighted time score could thus be obtained by multiplying the number of times *S* touched toys in each class, and the amount of time for which he handled them, by the appropriate weights.

The record sheet also listed the seven responses of the model that involved some highly specific manner of handling a toy. During the second period for which *E* was absent from the room, the observer placed a checkmark in the allocated space on the sheet each time *S* made a response that fitted the category. The total number of these responses given by each *S* provided the final set of data for analysis.

RESULTS

The form of the distributions of data provided by the latency, number-of-deviations, and time measures did not meet the requirements for parametric analyses; consequently, *S*s were ranked in respect to these and the weighted measures, and Kruskal-Wallis analyses of variance by ranks (Siegel, 1956) were utilized for testing the significance of differences among groups. Table 6.1 gives the median scores and mean ranks for each group of *S*s and the outcome of the tests. Comparisons between pairs of groups, using the three unweighted deviation measures, were made by means of Mann-Whitney U-tests (Table 6.2). These tests indicated that reward to the model and the absence of consequences both increased the probability of deviation, assuming that the "no-film" group provides a "baseline" level of response. There were no significant differences between the model-rewarded and no-consequence groups. The Ss who had seen the punishment movie deviated more quickly and exhibited more deviant behavior than the no-film group, but the differences between these two groups were not significant.

Twenty-one children did not deviate during E's 15-minute absence. The distribution of deviators and nondeviators among the four groups of subjects is given in Table 6.3.

Table 6.4 gives, for each group of children, the mean number of responses that were approximately the same as the seven distinctive play responses of the child in the movie. This table shows that responses of these kinds were not absent among the no-film children, but occurred with considerably greater frequency among children who had seen the film. The incidence of these responses was approximately the same in all three film groups.

DISCUSSION

Generally speaking, E's prohibition, although mild, appeared to be very effective for the children in this study. Of the no-film group, nearly half the children did not deviate at all; four more children deviated only once and then only for a very brief period. Deviations among the remainder of the children were rarely numerous or prolonged (Table 6.1). Consequently, it seems reasonable to assume that most or all children, because of their previous social-learning experiences, anticipated the possibility of receiving punishment for breaking the prohibition.

If the above assumption is made, the finding that children in the no-consequence group deviated as readily and as often as those in the model-rewarded group can perhaps be attributed to the nonoccurrence of punishment to the deviant model. According to Mowrer (1960a), an organism experiences "relief" when a danger signal terminates without the occurrence of the custom-

TABLE 6.1: *Group Medians and Mean Ranks on Five Indices of Resistance to Deviation*[a]

Index	Reward[c]		No consequences		Punishment		No Film		H[b]	p
	Median	Mean rank	Median	Mean rank	Median	Mean rank	Median	Mean rank		
Latency (seconds)	137	30	135	28.5	310	46	844	62	13.26	<0.005
No. deviations	3	51	3	51	2	39.5	1	27	13.84	<0.005
Time spent in deviation (seconds)	7	50	8	54	2	32.5	1	25.5	13.75	<0.005
Weighted No. deviations	4	58.5	3	48.5	2	38	1	27	14.13	<0.005
Weighted time	7	49.5	8	53	2	32	1	25.5	13.85	<0.005

[a] The smaller the value, the lower the rank.
[b] Corrected for ties.
[c] $n = 21$ in each group.

ary noxious stimulation; "relief is a form of secondary decremental reinforcement and ought, therefore, to be capable of counter-conditioning fear itself" (p. 419). A similar process may occur when an observer anticipates adverse consequences to a model and these consequences do not accrue. The observer's fear of punishment may be to some extent counterconditioned, resulting in an increased probability that the observer will himself perform, in a precisely or nonspecifically imitative manner, the classes of responses exhibited by the model.

The effect of the nonoccurrence of a positive reinforcer following a period of reinforcement has received considerable attention from learning theorists (for example, Amsel, 1958, 1962; Lawrence & Festinger, 1962); the function of "nonpunishment," i.e., no adverse consequences following actual or anticipated punishment, has been largely overlooked. A recent study by Virginia Crandall (1963) casts some light on the influence of

TABLE 6.2: *Significance of Differences between Reward-Film, No-Consequence Film, Punishment Film, and No-Film Groups on Three Measures of Resistance to Deviation[a]*

	Reward film vs. no-consequence film		Reward film vs. punishment film		Reward film vs. no film	
	z	p	z	p	z	p
Latency	0.09	n.s.	2.34	0.02	2.99	0.003
No. deviations	0.76	n.s.	2.43	0.02	3.14	0.002
Time spent in deviating	0.74	n.s.	2.24	0.03	3.12	0.002
	No-consequence film vs. punishment film		No-consequence film vs. no film		Punishment film vs. no film	
Latency	2.19	0.03	2.55	0.01	0.98	n.s.
No. deviations	1.73	0.08	2.66	0.008	1.05	n.s.
Time spent in deviating	1.76	0.08	2.55	0.01	1.04	n.s.

[a] Mann-Whitney U-test; normal approximation z-values were corrected for ties; all values are two-tailed.

TABLE 6.3: *Distribution of Subjects Who Did Not Deviate*[a]

Ss	Reward	no consequences	Punishment	No film
Deviated	19	19	14	11
Did not deviate	2	2	7	10

a Chi-square = 11.87; $p < 0.01$.

TABLE 6.4: *Mean Number of Play Responses Similar to Those of Model, after Removal of Prohibition*

Reward[a]		No consequences		Punishment		No film		F	p
Mean	SD	Mean	SD	Mean	SD	Mean	SD		
4.95	1.68	4.95	1.74	4.52	2.11	2.81	1.76	5.41	<0.005

a n = 21 in each group

the omission of direct punishment for a previously punished act. Crandall gave children the task of matching angles with a set of "standards." During the first twelve trials, one group of children received verbal approval on nine occasions; children in a second group were told on nine occasions that their responses were wrong; with a third group of children the experimenter said nothing. All three groups were then given a second set of trials, during which the experimenter remained silent. A measure of each child's expectancy of success was secured at the outset of the session and again after each of the two series of trials. The results of the study demonstrated that "nonreward" that followed reward decreased the children's expectancies of success whereas "nonreward" (or "nonpunishment") following punishment functioned in a precisely opposite manner.

Crandall, Good, and Crandall (1964) modified the design of Virginia Crandall's study to include a condition in which the experimenter was removed from the room during a second set of trials. In this way, it was possible to differentiate the effects of adult nonreaction from those of extinction (no adult nonreaction). The results of the earlier study were confirmed and, in addition, the changes produced by adult nonreaction were significantly greater than those produced by extinction. The authors concluded that adult nonreaction "acquires active, contrasting reinforcement value of the sign opposite to that of the adult's preceding verbal reinforcement."

Both vicariously experienced omission of anticipated punishment and adult nonreaction to previously punished behavior may, under some circumstances, have a disinhibitory effect on the social behavior of children. Increases in the doll-play aggression of children when a permissive (nonreacting) adult is present probably illustrate the disinhibitory effect of directly experienced adult nonreaction (Buss, 1961). In the no-consequence film of our study the adult did not return to the room; nevertheless, in view of the initial adult-child sequence, the adult's failure to return may have been interpreted as nonintervention. A further condition involving a film that displays the reentry of a non-reacting mother-figure is being employed in a current study of the influence of vicariously experienced response consequences.

Walters et al. (1963) reported that children who had seen a model-punished film deviated less often than children who had seen no film. In contrast, the present study yielded no significant differences between the model-punished and no-film groups. The discrepant findings may be in part attributable to a social-class difference. Both the no-film and the model-rewarded children in the earlier study deviated much more readily than the comparable groups in the present study. The former children came from a lower-class, downtown metropolitan area largely populated by an immigrant group known to be somewhat indulgent in their child-training practices. The latter children were either from middle-class suburbs of the metropolis or from a much smaller, more cohesive urban community. The *E*'s prohibition may consequently have been more effective for controlling the behavior of the children in the second study.

The finding that children in the model-punished group deviated more readily than children in the no-film group nevertheless merits an attempt at explanation. A clue is provided by the behavior of children who observed the no-consequences sequence. These children deviated relatively quickly and often, indicating that observation of the model's playing with the toys had in itself a disinhibitory effect. Children in the model-punished group saw precisely the same sequence as children in the no-consequence group with the addition of the punishment ending. Perhaps observation of the play of the subsequently punished model had an initially disinhibitory effect that was not fully counteracted by the punishing consequences to the model.

In the play period following renewal of the prohibition, children in all three film groups exhibited more responses similar to those displayed by the model than did children in the no-film group; more importantly, the three film groups differed little among themselves in the incidence of imitative behavior. This finding may be interpreted as indicating that vicariously experienced reinforcement has little or no effect on observational *learning,* but considerable effect on *performance.* However, one cannot be certain that under the conditions of this experiment the children in the film groups acquired any completely *novel* responses as a result of viewing the film. In other words, our experimental manipulations may have served only to modify the probabilities of performance of previously learned responses.

Moreover, the term "vicarious reinforcement" may obscure the noncomparability of the procedures employed in this study and those used in studies of the effects on behavior of directly administered social rewards and punishments. In the latter studies, pleasurable or aversive stimuli are continuously or intermittently presented on a *series* of occasions on which an instance of a specified class of responses occurs; such reinforcement procedures, it is generally agreed, primarily influence *learning,* i.e., the strength of the reinforced response class, rather than *performance,* which is largely a function of external cues and the drive or arousal level of the subject. Why, then, in our study should response consequences primarily influence performance? The answer may be that consequences of responses to a social model serve only as discriminative stimuli signifying to the observer the permissibility or nonpermissibility of a response class within a

given social context. The presentation of a specific kind of consequence certainly involves a modification of the total stimulus
complex that may result in the eliciting of a different hierarchy
of habits from that elicited when the consequence is omitted; yet,
no change in the relative strength of existing habits may occur. If
this analysis is correct, response consequences to a model have a
cue function but do not, strictly speaking, provide vicarious reinforcement; rather, they constitute a manipulation of the same
order as the experimenter's subsequent verbal removal of the
prohibition, which also influences performance. The absence of
differential effects for the reward and no-consequence conditions in the present study may, in this case, simply indicate that
the absence of adverse consequences was a sufficient condition
for the violation of a prohibition and that the addition of reward
involved no significant stimulus change.

In view of the large number of nondeviant cases, it might be
thought that resistance to deviation was largely an "all-or-none"
affair. Indeed, when analyses were made of the latency, number-of-deviations, and time measures for the 63 deviating subjects, the differences among groups failed to reach significance.
Nevertheless, these differences were in the direction predicted
and sufficiently large to argue against an "all-or-none" interpretation. Median scores for the reward, no-consequence, punishment, and no-film groups, respectively, were as follows: 120, 86,
236, and 264 seconds for latency; 4, 4, 3, and 2 for number of
deviations; and 11, 12, 2, and 1 seconds for time. The results for
deviating children therefore suggest that *strength* of resistance
was differentially influenced by the film sequences and that the
results would have been even more impressive had it been possible to continue each testing session until it was terminated by a
deviation. Unfortunately, it has not proved practical to keep
children of kindergarten and first grade ages for longer than 15
minutes under the "temptation" condition, since many nondeviators tend to become upset and unwilling to remain in the room
beyond this period of time. Future studies should probably be
carried out with older children, although more strongly established individual differences may make it necessary approxi-

mately to equate subjects for initial strength of resistance through pretraining procedures involving direct punishment for deviation.

R E F E R E N C E S

AMSEL, A. 1958. The role of frustrative nonreward in noncontinuous reward situations. *Psychological Bulletin,* 55, 102–119.

AMSEL, A. 1962. Frustrative nonreward in partial reinforcement and discrimination learning: Some recent history and a theoretical extension. *Psychological Review,* 69, 306–328.

BANDURA, A., ROSS, DOROTHEA, & ROSS, SHEILA A. 1963. Vicarious reinforcement and imitation. *Journal of Abnormal and Social Psychology,* 67, 601–607.

BANDURA, A., & WALTERS, R. H. 1963. *Social learning and personality development.* New York: Holt.

BUSS, A. H. 1961. *The psychology of aggression.* New York: Wiley.

CRANDALL, VIRGINIA C. 1963. Reinforcement effects of adult reactions and nonreactions on children's achievement expectations. *Child Development,* 34, 335–354.

CRANDALL, VIRGINIA C., GOOD, SUZANNE, & CRANDALL, V. J. 1964. Reinforcement effects of adult reactions and nonreactions on children's achievement expectations. A replication. *Child Development,* 35, 485–497.

HILL, W. F. 1960. Learning theory and the acquisition of values. *Psychological Review,* 67, 317–331.

LAWRENCE, D. H., & FESTINGER, L. 1962. *Deterrents and reinforcements: The psychology of insufficient rewards.* Stanford: Stanford University Press.

LEFKOWITZ, M. M., BLAKE, R. R., AND MOUTON, JANE S. 1955. Status factors in pedestrian violation of traffic signals. *Journal of Abnormal and Social Psychology,* 51, 704–706.

MOWRER, O. H. 1960a. *Learning theory and behavior.* New York: Wiley.

MOWRER, O. H. 1960b. *Learning theory and the symbolic processes.* New York: Wiley.

SIEGEL, S. 1956. *Nonparametric statistics for the behavioral sciences.* New York: McGraw-Hill.

WALTERS, R. H., & DEMKOW, LILLIAN. 1963. Timing of punishment as a determinant of response inhibition. *Child Development,* 34, 207–214.

WALTERS, R. H., & LLEWELLYN THOMAS, E. 1963. Enhancement of punitiveness by visual and audiovisual displays. *Canadian Journal of Psychology,* 17, 244–255.

WALTERS, R. H., LEAT, MARION, & MEZEI, L. 1963. Response inhibition and disinhibition through empathetic learning. *Canadian Journal of Psychology,* 17, 235–243.

7 *Imitation and Grammatical Development in Children*

DAN I. SLOBIN

A much-needed "new look" in studies of child language learning, stimulated by transformational grammar and characterized by the work of such psychologists as Roger Brown, Susan Ervin-Tripp, and Martin Braine, has emphasized the creative and original aspects of the child's learning, and has minimized the role of imitation, the traditionally overburdened explanatory device in this realm (Braine, 1963; Brown & Bellugi, 1964; Brown and Fraser, 1963; Chomsky, 1965; Ervin, 1964; Fraser, Bellugi, & Brown, 1963; Miller and Ervin, 1964). Discussions by linguists, and later by psychologists, have emphasized that linguistic competence can only be successfully characterized in terms of a system of rules which can generate the essentially infinite number of possible sentences of a language. If

From CONTEMPORARY ISSUES IN DEVELOPMENTAL PSYCHOLOGY edited by Norman S. Endler, Lawrence R. Boulter, and Harry Osser. Copyright © 1968 by Holt, Rinehart and Winston, Inc. Reprinted by permission of Holt, Rinehart and Winston, Inc.

a child were to spend a lifetime imitating the sentences he heard, we could never account for the outstanding ability of every human being to speak and understand sentences he has clearly never heard before but which are nevertheless acceptable as sentences of his language. And, indeed, recent careful observers of child language have heard the child speak many utterances which he could never have heard—which could not be imitations or reduced imitations of adult utterances—but which seem to be explainable in terms of an inferred structure, in terms of the child's idiosyncratic grammar. For example, drawing from the studies of Braine (1963) and Brown and his co-workers (Brown & Bellugi, 1964), we have utterances like: *allgone pacifier, put on it,* and *a this truck.* Such examples are simply a more dramatic way of making the same point: almost all utterances are novel.

Limitations of imitation-based models of language learning are further underscored by the work of Eric Lenneberg (1962), who brought to our attention the case of a boy who, for physiological reasons, could never utter a word, yet learned to understand the complexities of English grammar and semantics; and the cases of mongoloid children, who speak much yet do not fully master these complexities (Lenneberg et al., 1964). Imitation, then, is certainly not *necessary* in learning to understand, nor does it ensure learning to speak. But is there any evidence that at least it can *help*—that at least it can help a *normal* child in learning the grammar of this language?*

One way of posing this question is to ask if a child can say anything in imitation that he cannot say spontaneously. Can he speak sentences which are longer or more complicated than he usually does if he is given an immediately preceding model from an adult?

Roger Brown and his associates have worked with elicited imitations. He and Colin Fraser (1963) asked six children, between

---

* I am concerned here with the role of imitation in grammatical development only; it may function as a more significant learning device in other domains, such as the child's learning of pronunciation and of new vocabulary items and clichés.

the ages of 25 and 35 months, to repeat sentences after the experimenter, and found the mean lengths of such imitations to be about equal to the mean lengths of these children's spontaneous utterances, and to have the same "telegraphic" character. These two investigators, working together with Ursula Bellugi (Fraser, Bellugi, & Brown, 1963), found, however, that children between the ages of 37 and 43 months could imitate sentences which they could not comprehend and which they could not produce on their own. So, in looking at these experiments with *elicited* limitations, we find that until they reach a certain age, children can do no better in imitating than in speaking.

Susan Ervin-Tripp has rightly objected that Brown's children were *asked* to imitate, while a better test "as to whether imitation is significant as a source of progress in grammer should be based on spontaneous imitations, for children may imitate selectively" (Ervin, 1964, p. 164). She and Wick Miller (Miller & Ervin, 1964) have worked intensively with five children between the ages of 22 and 34 months—about the same age range as Brown and Fraser's younger group. This study led Ervin-Tripp to the forthright conclusion that "there is not a shred of evidence supporting a view that progress toward adult norms of grammar arises merely from practice in overt imitation of adult sentences" (Ervin, 1964, p. 172). Roughly, what she did was to grammatically analyze the children's free speech—the things they said on their own—and determine if their spontaneous imitations were any more complex grammatically than their free speech. Overall, she found no differences in complexity. Menyuk (1963), too, has found that little children tend to use their own grammars when producing repetitions of adult model sentences under conditions of elicited imitation. Such findings certainly cast strong doubt on the supposition that imitation can be considered a useful explanatory device in accounting for the child's syntactic development.

Careful examination of another sort of data, however, hints that there may yet be a slight shred of evidence that a specific sort of imitation could play some role in this process. Ervin-

Tripp's data are not completely natural, just as Brown's earlier data are not, for though she and Miller did their work in the children's homes, and studied spontaneous rather than elicited imitations, the situation was not a usual one for the child: he was interacting with adult experimenters rather than with his mother. Perhaps there is a special aspect of mother-child dialogue which is not revealed in this situation.

Roger Brown's group at Harvard has been carefully following two children, appropriately nicknamed "Adam and Eve" in the literature (Brown & Bellugi, 1964), from about 18 months to three years of age. In examining the transcripts of these sessions, recorded in a normal home situation, it has become clear to me that one cannot simply speak of spontaneous imitations, or the overall role of imitation as a single process. Imitation plays many roles, and these roles may vary at different ages. The child repeats new words he hears, he repeats questions and commands, he repeats praise, he repeats adults' descriptions of what is going on, he repeats playfully, and so on. It becomes necessary to look at the many different sorts of situations in which a child imitates—and we need not expect them all to be grammatically progressive.

If you take a very fine-grained view of grammatical development (Brown, personal communication) you often find that a given construction appears first as an imitation of a parent's utterance, and only several weeks or months later as part of the child's own spontaneous speech. Here we seem to have evidence which goes against Ervin-Tripp's findings—imitations *can* be grammatically progressive.

What I am especially interested in, though, are those special situations in which the child repeats an adult's response to his own speech. Adults tend to "expand" the child's utterances very frequently (Brown & Bellugi, 1964). If you listen to adults and children together you will often hear the *adult* imitating what the *child* says—but, in so doing, the adult fills in the child's telegraphic speech and clarifies it; makes it into a full sentence. For example, a child might say, "Play Momma slipper," and the other will reply, "Play with Momma's slipper," adding a preposition and an inflection. Or a child may say, "Play piano," and the mother will say something like, "playing the piano," adding an inflection and an article. Sometimes these expansions are given with a declarative intonation, as if the adult were simply confirming what the child has said. And sometimes they are given with a rising intonation; for example, the child may say, "Oh no raining," and the mother may ask, "Oh no, it's not raining?" These "expansion-questions" appear to be a sort of communication check—the mother offers an expansion and seems to ask: "Is this what you had in mind?"

The speech of very young children has a peculiar force in eliciting these sorts of expanded imitations from adults. As Brown and Bellugi point out: "Indeed we found it very difficult to withhold expansions. A reduced or incomplete English sentence seems to constrain the English-speaking adult to expand it into the nearest properly formed complete sentence" (p. 144). In fact, about 30 percent of the utterances of Adam and Eve called forth expansions from their mothers. Interestingly enough, the mothers "imitated" their children about *three times* as frequently as they themselves were imitated, for only about 10 percent of the children's utterances were spontaneous imitations of adults. Figures like these drive one to examine the process in search of a function.

The special imitation situation I am concerned with here is the child's imitation of these expansions. This happens fairly frequently: about 15 percent of the children's imitations in Brown's transcripts are repetitions of expansions or responses to expansion-questions. The further question, of course, is whether children benefit from this sort of imitation of an expansion. Note that in so doing there are three things a child can do: *(a)* he can simply repeat his original utterance, without picking up anything the adult added to it; or *(b)* he can say something even shorter than what he started out to say; or, most interestingly, *(c)* he can add something to his original utterance, something he picked up from the expansion. For example, the child says, "Papa name Papa."

Then the mother expands, "Papa's name is Papa, um-hum." And the child repeats this expansion: "Papa name is Papa." Here he has added something—the copular verb which is usually lacking in his own speech. This third option is the most popular for Adam and Eve: they take it about 50 percent of the time when imitating expansions, as shown in Table 7.1

Here is a situation, I believe, where imitation may be capable of helping the child advance in his grammatical development. When Adam and Eve expanded their original utterances in imitating adult expansions they added such items as the article, the copula, a pronoun, a preposition, an inflection—just those things generally missing in their own telegraphic speech. These utterances, if not beyond the child's spontaneous capacities, at least stretch those capacities to their limit. One often has the impression that the young child has a severely limited span in speaking —that he can only make so many decisions per sentence—and that an expansion, immediately following his speech, and in the same situation, can stretch this span slightly.

The sentence-programming span I refer to here is not so much

TABLE 7.1: *Imitations of Expansions*

TYPE OF IMITATION	EXAMPLE	RELATIVE FREQUENCY*	
		Adam	Eve
(a) Unexpanded	*Child:* "Just like cowboy." *Adult:* "Oh, just like the cowboy's." *Child:* "Just like cowboy."	45%	17%
(b) Reduced	*Child:* "Play piano." *Adult:* "Playing the piano." *Child:* "Piano."	7%	29%
(c) Expanded	*Child:* "Pick 'mato." *Adult:* "Picking tomatoes up?" *Child:* "Pick 'mato up."	49%	54%

* These figures cover Adam from age 2,3 to 2,10 and Eve from 1,6 to 2,2.

a matter of length as a matter of the number of operations involved in generating a sentence. Ursula Bellugi has cogent examples from Adam's speech (personal communication). For example, when Adam had mastered the possessive inflection in such simple statements as "Daddy's chair," he omitted it in more complicated constructions such as "Where Daddy chair?" Or, when he had learned to invert the auxiliary for yes-no questions, such as "Can't it be a bigger truck?" and "Can I go out?", he still failed to perform this operation in the case of more complex questions like "Why he can go there?"

It could be that the opportunity to imitate expansions is especially helpful in such cases, where the child can use a given operation if not distracted by additional syntactic complexity. And, more broadly, expansions would seem to be an excellent natural teaching device. The mother gives the child a correct model for his own speech, at a time when his attention is engaged, and in which the semantic content—the situation—remains unchanged. Brown and Bellugi go on to the intriguing suggestion that, in providing a child with the "little words" and grammatical markers—the functors which are missing from his telegraphic speech —a mother may be guiding him (to use Whorf's picturesque phrase) to "dissect nature along lines laid down by our native languages":

> The expansion encodes aspects of reality that are not coded by the child's telegraphic utterance. Functors have meaning, but it is meaning that accrues to them in context rather than isolation. The meanings that are added by functors seem to be nothing less than the basic terms in which we construe reality: the time of an action, whether it is ongoing or completed, whether it is presently relevant or not; the concept of possession, and such relational concepts as are coded by *in, on, up, down,* and the like; the difference between a particular instance of a class ("Has anybody seen *the* paper?") and any instance of a class ("Has anybody seen *a* paper?"); the difference between extended substances given shape and size by an "accidental" container (*sand, water, syrup,* etc.) and countable "things" having a characteristic, fixed shape and size (*a cup, a man, a tree,* etc.). It seems to us that a

mother, in expanding speech, may be teaching more than grammar; she may be teaching something like a world view (1964, pp. 147–148).

Changes with age in the use of imitations and expansions are also suggestive. On the basis of the transcripts of Adam and Eve it appears that as a child grows older he imitates less, and the surrounding adults expand his speech less often. Early on, interchanges between mother and child very often look rather as if each one were trying to figure out what the other one is trying to say. Many of the child's earlier imitations have a rising intonation, as in the following interchange between Adam and his mother when he was about two-and-a-half years old:

Mother:	"It fits in the puzzle someplace."
Adam:	"Puzzle? Puzzle someplace?"
Mother:	"Turn it around."
Adam:	"Turn around?"
Mother:	"No, the other way."
Adam:	"Other way?"
Mother:	"I guess you have to turn it around."
Adam:	"Guess turn it round. Turn round."

By about age three mother and child seem to be conversing much more with each other, rather than imitating each other. This is a striking difference between the earlier and later transcripts. Apparently the mother stops expanding because the child's utterances have become fuller—it is now easier to guess what he means, and conversation becomes more and more possible. In interchanges now the mother's sentences are follow-up sentences, as in adult conversation, rather than expansions. And, of course, at the same time, the child's opportunity to imitate expansions also disappears—but his rate of imitation generally has dropped to only two or three percent by this time anyway.

All of these findings and speculations give me the feeling that there may be some sort of "critical age" for expansions—an age when the child is most helped with an expanded model of his own utterance to imitate (either overtly, or perhaps, covertly).

This is an age at which he is just able to say more than he usually does, but often does not do so. It may also be an age when, for a variety of reasons, he may be especially prone to imitate. This seems to find some support when one looks at changes with age in the imitations of Adam and Eve. In the earliest sample, when Eve was 18 months old, 13 percent of her utterances were imitations. This percentage drops steadily. By the oldest age which I have tabulated—Adam at 34 months—the rate has dropped to 2 percent. There are also clear changes with age in the repetitions of expansions. Reduced repetitions drop out at an early age; unexpanded repetitions somewhat later; and expanded repetitions remain in evidence for a longer amount of time and are thus prevalent at a later age.

As suggestive as the entire preceding train of argument may be, however, we have virtually no evidence that adult expansions of child speech play any essential or even facilitative role in normal grammatical development. Indeed, the only study I know of which has attempted to deal with this issue has failed to substantiate the argument. Courtney Cazden, in a recent doctoral dissertation at Harvard (1965), worked daily for 12 weeks with 12 lower-class Negro children in a day-care center. The beginning ages of the children ranged from 28 to 38 months. Their speech was telegraphic, and its grammatical structure was carefully assessed before and after the three-month study. A control group of four children received no special treatment. The remaining eight children were placed in two equal experimental groups— "expansion" and "modeling." Individual children in these groups had daily sessions of 30–40 minutes with an adult. In one case, the adult always expanded every utterance of the child, following Brown and Bellugi's rule: "Retain the words given in the order given, and add those functors that will result in a well-formed simple sentence that is appropriate to the circumstances" (1964, p. 147. In the other case the child's speech was never expanded, but "modeled." Cazden defines a model as "any well-formed sentence (in response to a child's utterance) which does not contain the content words of the previous child utterance" (p. 42). Some of her examples of modeling are:

Child:	"I got apples."
Adult:	"Do you like them?"
Child:	"His name Tony."
Adult:	"That's right."
Child:	"We got some more."
Adult:	"There's a lot in there."*

The issue here, of course, is to determine which aspects of adult-child dialogue are especially facilitative to grammatical development. Cazden expected to find that both expansion and modeling would result in greater grammatical development in comparison with the control group, but that expansion would be the superior technique. Her data suggest, however, that while both forms of dialogue may be helpful, modeling alone is of considerably greater value than expanding alone. The order of grammatical improvement scores for the three groups is generally (1) modeling, (2) expansion, (3) control. In fact, examining all of her data, Cazden concludes: "There is no evidence that expansions, as provided in this research, aid the acquisition of grammar. All indications without exception, suggest that modeling is the more effective treatment" (p. vi).

The problem in interpreting Cazden's findings—in addition to the smallness of the sample—is that neither constant expansion nor constant withholding of expansion is a natural form of adult-child dialogue. Cazden concludes:

The only explanation I can offer is that as the concentration of expansions goes up—in this case far above that naturally occurring in parent-child conversation—the richness of the verbal

* It is interesting that Cazden found, as pointed out above, that it is exceedingly difficult for an adult to hold back the impulse to expand childish speech:

"What makes modeling without expanding difficult is that a child's telegraphic utterance seems to be a stimulus to which the attentive adult responds spontaneously with an expansion. The tutors could and did suppress the response deliberately, but the process remained unnatural. . . . And evident only on the tape recordings is the tell-tale pause when the listener can almost 'hear' the automatic expansion being suppressed and an alternative utterance improvised. Deliberate non-expansion can be recommended only as an experimental technique" (p. 43).

stimulation goes down. Expansions are by definition contingent on the child's speech in content as well as in timing. To the extent that they are pure expansions, just filling in the child's telegraphic utterance to make a complete sentence, they will have less variety of vocabulary and grammatical patterns than the adult's non-expanding speech normally contains. The suggestions that the richness-impoverishment dimension may be critical thus gains some support (p. 91).

What we need, then, is a systematic comparison of modeling alone, as opposed to a mix of both modeling and expansion. It has been suggested that frequency of parental expansion of child speech may be related to such variables as social class and education, and, in turn, be partly responsible for differences in language acquisition and ability in children of different socioeconomic backgrounds. The issue is certainly complex, and we are far from being able to determine the functions—if any—of expansion and imitation in the human child's remarkable acquisition of language. Until the necessary data are amassed, I would still like to believe that when a child hears an adult expansion of his own speech he learns something important about the structure of his language.

R E F E R E N C E S

BRAINE, M. D. S. 1963. The ontogeny of English phrase structure: The first phase. *Language,* 39, 1–13.

BROWN, R., & BELLUGI, URSULA. 1964. Three processes in the child's acquisition of syntax. In E. H. Lenneberg (Ed.), *New directions in the study of language.* Cambridge, Mass.: M. I. T. Press. Pp. 131–161. (Also in *Harvard Educational Review,* 34, 133–151.)

BROWN, R., & FRASER, C. 1963. The acquisition of syntax. In C. N. Cofer and Barbara S. Musgrave (Eds.), *Verbal behavior and learning: Problems and processes.* New York: McGraw-Hill. Pp. 158–197.

CAZDEN, COURTNEY B. 1965. Environmental assistance to the child's acquisition of grammar. Unpublished doctoral dissertation, Harvard University.

CHOMSKY, N. 1965. *Aspects of the theory of syntax.* Cambridge, Mass.: M. I. T. Press.

ERVIN, SUSAN M. 1964. Imitation and structural change in children's language. In E. H. Lenneberg (Ed.), *New directions in the study of language.* Cambridge, Mass.: M. I. T. Press. Pp. 163–189.

FRASER, C., BELLUGI, URSULA, & BROWN, R. 1963. Control of grammar in imitation, comprehension, and production. *Journal of Verbal Learning and Verbal Behavior, 2,* 121–135.

LENNEBERG, E. H. 1962. Understanding language without ability to speak: A case report. *Journal of Abnormal and Social Psychology, 65,* 419–425.

LENNEBERG, E. H., NICHOLS, IRENE A., & ROSENBERGER, ELEANOR F. 1964. Primitive stages of language development in mongolism. *Proceedings of the Association for Research in Nervous and Mental Disease, 42,* 119–137.

MENYUK, PAULA. 1963. A preliminary evaluation of grammatical capacity in children. *Journal of Verbal Learning and Verbal Behavior, 2,* 429–439.

MILLER, W. R., & ERVIN, SUSAN M. 1964. The development of grammar in child language. In Ursula Bellugi and R. Brown (Eds.), The acquisition of language. *Monographs of the Society for Research in Child Development, 29(1),* 9–33.

8 Effects of Age and Rule Familiarity on the Production of Modeled Language Constructions

ROBERT M. LIEBERT

RICHARD D. ODOM

JAE H. HILL

RAY L. HUFF

A recent study (Bandura & Harris, 1967) examined the effects of several social-learning variables on children's production of two syntactic constructions. The results demonstrated that those children exposed to a combination of *(a)* an adult model's production of sentences with and without the relevant construction, *(b)* reward for sentences containing the relevant construction, and *(c)* attention-focusing instructions showed a greater increment in the production of these constructions (passive or prepositional phrases) in their own sentences than did a control group.

With a slight modification of these procedures, Odom, Liebert, and Hill (1968) performed two experiments designed to provide additional information on the language productions of second-grade children. In the first of these experiments, children were exposed to and rewarded for the production of sentences containing familiar prepositional phrases of the form *preposition-article-noun,* while another group was exposed to and rewarded for the production of sentences containing unfamiliar prepositional constructions of the form *article-noun-preposition,* (for example, "the goat was *the door at"*). Surprisingly, both groups demonstrated an increase in the frequency of preposition-article-noun phrases (the familiar construction) relative to the performance of a control group which experienced no active model or reward. In the second experiment children in both experimental groups were asked to repeat verbatim the relevant sentences of the model immediately after they were rewarded. Even with the addition of this manipulation, spontaneous production of unfamiliar constructions was negligible. As before, the frequency of familiar constructions increased during training in both groups, but the repetition manipulation did not facilitate spontaneous productions over those made by either group in the first experiment. Children in the familiar group successfully repeated more of the model's rewarded sentences than did those in the unfamiliar group, although all children in the latter group were able to repeat correctly some of the model's rewarded, unfamiliar constructions.

The combined results of these experiments suggest that the children's adoption of language rules may have involved active and complex problem-solving strategies. The performance of the subjects exposed to unfamiliar constructions supports this conclusion. Instead of abstracting a new rule from the model's productions, the subjects in these conditions apparently reordered the unfamiliar language constructions to make them correspond

Reprinted by permission of the publisher from DEVELOPMENTAL PSYCHOLOGY, 1969, Vol. 1, pp. 108–112. Copyright 1969, American Psychological Association.

Grateful acknowledgment is made to the teachers and officials of the Jack and Jill School, Reeves Kindergarten, and Seven Hills Swimming Club, without whose generous cooperation this study would not have been possible.

to language rules with which they were familiar. If the subjects perceive the situation as a problem-solving task, then the reordering phenomenon may be viewed as one of several possible strategies. This strategy, which involves a previously learned language rule, apparently prevailed over a host of alternatives, including the one leading to the "correct" solution.

There are two alternative explanations for this reordering phenomenon which suggest differential predictions regarding the performance of subjects both older and younger than those previously used. Specifically, if reordering of unfamiliar constructions is due primarily to the child's prior experience with the English language, then successful repetition and spontaneous production of sentences which deviate from familiar language rules should *decrease* with *increasing age*. If, on the other hand, the reordering strategy represents an inability to abstract the new rule in a relatively brief training period, then successful repetition and production of the new construction might be thought to represent a strategy which is made possible by the development of abstraction processes. If one assumes that the cognitive changes which occur with development involve the increased functioning of such processes, then the strategy of repeating and producing the unfamiliar construction would be expected to *increase* with *increasing age*. The major purpose of the present experiment was to compare these alternative formulations.

Method

Subjects

The subjects were 84 white children of average intelligence who were enrolled in private summer recreational programs serving comparable middle-class sections of Nashville. Seven boys and seven girls from three age groups (chronological ages, CA, 5.8, 8.4, and 14.1) were assigned to each of the treatments.

Within each age level, subjects were further balanced between treatments as closely as possible with respect to CA.

Verbal Stimuli

As in a previous study, the verbal stimuli were 95 nouns which are commonly known by children of the youngest age used (Rinsland, 1945). Fifty-five of these nouns were chosen for the subjects, and 40 for the model (M). The experimenter read the stimulus nouns to both the subject and M.

Procedure

Each subject was brought individually to a mobile laboratory by the experimenter, an adult male, and introduced to M, also an adult male. The experimenter told each subject that he was interested in the ways that people make up sentences, and indicated that he was also interested in comparing the sentences of children and adults. Each subject was also told that the sentences he produced did not have to be true, and that they could be either statements or questions.

An equal number of boys and girls in each age group were assigned to each of two conditions. The procedures common to both conditions were *(a)* some preliminary trials in which M and the subject constructed sentences to insure that all subjects understood the task, *(b)* a base-rate period during which the subject constructed 10 sentences, and *(c)* a training period during which the subject constructed 20 sentences and M produced 30. If the subject was unable to use any word in a sentence after 1 minute, the experimenter proceeded to the next noun.

At the end of the base-rate period the experimenter explained that he liked some sentences better than others, and advised M and the subject to pay close attention to those sentences which he would indicate were especially good. Both M and the subject were generously praised by the experimenter (for example, "I like that sentence" or "very good") for sentences containing relevant prepositional constructions. Additionally, in order to enhance the subject's discrimination of the relevant constructions, the experimenter gave the subject a token immediately after each of his relevant sentences and told him that these tokens could be traded for a prize at the end of the task.

For the familiar English rule (ER) condition, relevant sentences were those containing grammatical prepositional phrases of the form preposition-article-noun, for example, "The boy went *to the house.*" During training M produced 22 relevant sentences and 8 irrelevant sentences. The latter contained no prepositional phrases and were randomly interspersed among the relevant sentences so as to provide an opportunity for the subject to discriminate the relevant construction. To further enhance this discrimination, the prepositional phrases were always at the end of

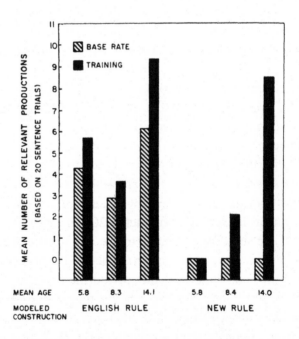

FIGURE 8.1. Mean production of relevant prepositional constructions during base rate and training in all experimental groups

the sentence and the subject was asked to repeat those of M's sentences which contained the relevant construction. The M generated 15 sentences immediately after the subject completed the base-rate period and then alternated with the subject in blocks of five trials until the subject had generated his 20 sentences. The unfamiliar or new rule (NR) condition had ungrammatical prepositional phrases of the form article-noun-preposition, for example, "The boy went *the house to.*" M's sentences were memorized to insure that the modeling cues were the same for all subjects within treatments. The sentences were all either six or seven words in length.

All of the subject's sentences were recorded verbatim on tape, from which frequencies of prepositional phrases fitting the two rules for both the base-rate and training phases were subsequently tallied.

RESULTS

Increments in Relevant Constructions

Of particular interest in this study was the influence of rule familiarity and age upon increments in the subjects' production of sentences which precisely fitted the modeled rule. Since all subjects had 10 base-rate trials and 20 training trials, difference scores were computed by doubling each subject's base-rate production for relevant prepositional constructions and then subtracting this transformed score from his training score for that construction. Preliminary analyses revealed no significant sex differences. The data for both sexes were therefore combined for all analyses. Figure 8.1 presents the mean transformed base-rate and training scores for relevant constructions in each of the six experimental groups.

Since marked heterogeneity of variance was noted among the groups, an analysis of variance was performed on square-root transformed difference scores. This analysis revealed a highly significant effect for age ($F = 10.54$, $p < .0001$), whereas only trends were found for rule familiarity ($F = 3.67$, $p < .1$) and the Rule $\times$ Age interaction ($F = 2.67$, $p < .1$). Individual comparisons indicated that the oldest age group showed significantly greater increments than either the middle ($t = 3.20$, $p < .01$, two-tailed) or youngest groups ($t = 4.00$, $p < .001$, two-tailed), while the increments shown by the two younger groups did not differ ($t = .80$). Further, as seen in Figure 8.1, both the trend for NR superiority and for a Rule $\times$ Age interaction appear to be accounted for by the impressive improvement of the oldest children in the NR group.

Production of ER Constructions by NR Groups

Previous research (Odom et al., 1968) found that subjects in the NR condition showed an increment in their production of grammatical constructions. To determine the degree to which this phenomenon again appeared in the present study, difference scores based on ER constructions made during base rate and training by subjects in the NR groups at each of the three age levels were computed. The data revealed that children in the youngest group tended to behave like those in the previous study, showing an increment in the production of grammatically correct, but nonrelevant constructions ($x = 1.43$, $t = 1.61$, $p < .1$, one-tailed). In contrast, children in the middle and oldest age groups both showed a mean decrease in these grammatically correct constructions ($x = -2.93$, $t = 3.62$, $p < .01$; $x = -5.64$, $t = 4.27$, $p < .005$, respectively, two-tailed).

Accuracy of Repetitions

It will be recalled that all children were asked to repeat the rewarded sentences of the M to whom they were exposed. In the ER conditions, subjects in the two oldest groups were able to repeat all of M's sentences without a single exception, and subjects in the youngest group failed to repeat accurately only an average of 1 of M's 22 rewarded sentences. In contrast, for subjects in the NR conditions repetition was somewhat less accurate for all three age groups. The youngest and middle-age groups failed to repeat an average of 4.3 and 4.8 sentences, respectively, while the mean number of incorrect sentence repetitions for the oldest subjects in the NR condition was 1.8. An analysis of variance revealed that there were fewer repetition errors made in the ER than in the NR group ($F = 41.55, p < .001$) and that the oldest group made fewer errors than the two younger groups ($F = 4.60, p > .025$).

An inspection of the repetition errors in the NR condition indicated that most were reordered forms of the modeled NR constructions. Reordering took the form of either preposition-article-noun (ER construction) or preposition-article-noun-preposition. Reordered constructions accounted for 70% of the youngest group's repetition errors, 66% of the middle-age group's errors, and 68% of the oldest group's errors.

Discussion

The results of this experiment lend additional support to the general hypothesis that children's adoption of language rules may be influenced by a combination of modeling and reward procedures and provide data concerning the relationship of this influence to age. In the ER condition, the findings partially confirmed the hypothesis that the ability to abstract and subsequently employ a language rule exemplified in the sentences of a social model is directly related to the age of the subjects. Thus, the performance of the oldest children was superior to that of either of the two younger groups.

With respect to the performance of children in the NR condition, it will be recalled that two alternative formulations were considered. It is apparent from the data that familiarity with

English grammar (which presumably covaries with age) does not impede children's ability to abstract and use a novel and unfamiliar grammatical rule. Instead, accomplishing this task is apparently facilitated by age, as suggested by the developmental problem-solving hypothesis with respect to the learning of unfamiliar language rules. Thus, unlike the previous studies conducted within a social learning framework (e.g., Bandura & Harris, 1967; Odom et. al., 1968), the present study provides direct information about the *acquisition* of novel language rules and suggests that these can be imparted by a combination of modeling and reward variables.

With respect to the repetition data, the anticipated differences between the ER and NR conditions were also obtained. Not surprisingly, ER children in all three age groups showed nearly perfect repetition of M's rewarded sentences. In contrast, children in the NR group had difficulty with repetitions and, consistent with other performance findings, the younger NR groups experienced the greatest difficulty. As noted, the preponderance of erroneous repetitions were characterized by a reordering of the components of the prepositional phrase in the direction of greater correspondence to English grammar. This finding, too, appears to provide corroboration for the suggestion that language learning and performance may be fruitfully viewed as problem-solving tasks.

Most interesting is the fact that the oldest children showed greater increments in relevant constructions in the NR than in the ER condition. In fact, as seen in Figure 8.1, their training performance is no poorer than that of their counterparts who were exposed to a familiar English construction. The authors have previously noted the possibility that the novelty of the NR constructions might provide a basis for readily discriminating them as compared with the grammatical prepositional constructions modeled in the ER group. The present finding provides some support for this interpretation, but its generality is apparently limited to children with sufficient cognitive skills to process this novel information accurately.

REFERENCES

BANDURA, A., & HARRIS, M. B. 1967. Modification of syntactic style. *Journal of Experimental Child Psychology,* 4, 341–352.

ODOM, R. D., LIEBERT, R. M., & HILL, J. H. 1968. The effects of modeling cues, reward, and attentional set on the production of grammatical and ungrammatical syntactic constructions. *Journal of Experimental Child Psychology,* 6, 131–140.

RINSLAND, H. 1945. *A basic vocabulary of elementary school children.* New York: Macmillan.

9

Observationally Induced Changes in Children's Interrogative Classes

TED L. ROSENTHAL
BARRY J. ZIMMERMAN
KATHLEEN DURNING

Curiously little research in the social-learning tradition has been directed toward concept formation or abstract categorization. Traditionally, developmental issues of selecting and grouping, and the evolution of cognitive classifications (for example, the abstraction of common stimulus properties from different objects), have been the particular concerns of organismi-

Reprinted by permission of the publisher from the JOURNAL OF PERSONALITY AND SOCIAL PSYCHOLOGY, 1970, Vol. 16, pp. 681–688. Copyright 1970, American Psychological Association.

This study was supported by the Arizona Center for Early Childhood Education and was performed pursuant to a contract with the United States Office of Education, Department of Health, Education, and Welfare. The authors wish to acknowledge the generous cooperation of Principals E. B. Appleman, W. F. Braucher, C. E. Lopez, and S. Polito, of their teachers, and of the administration of Tucson School District I. They are grateful to Albert Bandura, Wayne R. Carroll, Clinton L. Trafton, and Glenn M. White for their helpful suggestions regarding the manuscript.

cally oriented scholars (cf. Baldwin, 1968). Although one might anticipate that higher order conceptual phenomena could be modified by observing another person's responses, to date few studies based on a social-learning position have involved abstract or rule-governed cognitive behavior.

Bandura and McDonald (1963) have shown that modeling can influence a child's moral judgments toward criteria different from his original disposition, and these results have been replicated by Cowan, Langer, Heavenrich, and Nathanson (1969). Recently, social language learning research has demonstrated model-induced changes in the use of passive and prepositional linguistic constructions (Bandura & Harris, 1966; Odom, Liebert, & Hill, 1968) and in the parameters of verb tense and kernel sentence structure (Carroll, Rosenthal, & Brysh, 1969; Rosenthal & Whitebook, 1970).

The emphasis of all the foregoing experiments has been to demonstrate that particular linguistic structures, or judgmental criteria, were subject to social modification. Attention was not directed to transmitting a range of conceptually different, rule-governed dimensions by providing separate groups with varied instances of quite diverse, abstract criteria for organizing stimuli. Thus, within the language categories of tense or passive constructions, the range of instances is, relatively, constrained. When, for example, the model produced the past progressive (for example, *was pushing*), all his instances had to include the "was" auxiliary and the "-ing" inflection, thereby constraining stimulus diversity. Furthermore, little, if any, controlled experimentation has been devoted to the development or modification of information-seeking behavior. By means of the interrogative mood, one can both *solicit* information about the world, and *control,* or designate, the aspects or dimensions of events which comprise appropriate response to one's query; accordingly, information seeking would appear to merit study.

The present experiments investigated a model's influence upon children's formulation of questions regarding a set of stimulus pictures. Separate groups of children observed varied instances of questions representing one of four abstract classes. From the instances displayed, it was possible to *induce* the general properties of that class of questions which the child observed. The classes of questions studied pertained, alternatively, to the identity or physical attributes of the stimuli; to their pragmatic function; to causal relationships involving the stimuli; and to judgments of value or preference concerning the stimuli. Subsequent to the modeling phase, and without further performance by the model, a new set of stimulus pictures was introduced to assess generalization of information-seeking categories.

The four question classifications presently studied were intended to exemplify widely divergent rule-governed dimensions for the conceptual organization of a set of stimuli. Additionally, the question classes did provide partial overlap with Piaget's (1959) descriptive classification of children's questions. Thus, Piaget's "why" group of questions would all fall within our category of causal relationships concerning stimuli, as would Piaget's "questions of causal explanation." Piaget's "questions of classification and valuation" have, in the present procedure, been partitioned between nominal or physical stimulus properties, and judgments of value or preference regarding stimuli. Indeed, Piaget's definition of valuation ("the judgment of value," 1959, p. 217) is identical with that governing the present category of value questions.

METHOD

Subjects

From sixth-grade classes in four schools in Tucson, Arizona, 70 boys and 70 girls were randomly drawn and assigned to experimental or control variations. The children ranged in age from 11 to 13 years and represented disadvantaged populations, with a high proportion of Mexican-American youngsters in the sample. All schools from which subjects were drawn were receiving federal assistance under Title I funds for impacted areas. To each experimental variation, and to the control group, 14 boys and 14 girls were randomly assigned.

Materials and Model's Questions

Two parallel but different sets of 12 stimuli each were prepared; in each set, items adapted and redrawn from the Van Alstyne Picture Vocabulary Test (showing one achromatic common object, for example, a typewriter, per card) were successively alternated with unpublished items developed by the Demonstration and Research Center for Early Education, Peabody College (showing three variously colored common objects, for example, a yellow balloon, a yellow banana, and a red apple, per card). Thus, within each set of stimulus pictures, consecutive items varied in number, color, and pictorial contents. The first set of pictures was displayed to all subjects in each experiment during baseline, was the vehicle for the model's questions in the experimental variations, and was reexposed to all subjects to assess imitative (and control group) changes. The second set of pictures was subsequently displayed without modeling to *all* subjects, to assess generalization of question formulation.

Independent of assignment to experimental question class, the model's questions always involved 12 diverse instances of the criteria governing a class. Thus, for the experiment involving nominal physical questions, the model's questions included: "What shape is that?" and "Is that made of wood?" For the functional uses variation, the model's questions included: "What do you use it for?" and "Could you put water in this?" For the causal relations variation, the model's questions included: "When does the bell on the typewriter ring?" and "How come the guitar makes music?" For the value judgments variation, the model's questions include: "Which do you think is the prettiest?"

and "What do you like about this?" The complete set of the model's questions for each experiment is provided elsewhere.

For each experimental variation, responses were coded as representing instances of the model's question classes or as "other"; thus, within each question variation, the subjects' baseline, imitation, and generalization scores comprised the number of responses falling into the model's question category. For control subjects, the baseline, imitation, and generalization frequencies of response were separately scored for each question category to determine if the control group had shown any "spontaneous" changes from baseline to imitation or generalization retests within the separate question categories.

Pilot testing had established interscorer agreement exceeding 95% of utterances, and consequently, only one scorer coded the response data. The assignment of utterances to response categories proved relatively easy, and scoring problems were noted only in some 3% of responses; these difficult instances were resolved by discussion among the authors.

Design and Procedure

For each experiment, half of the subjects of each sex were randomly assigned to *implicit* or *explicit* modeling instructions treatments; thus, seven boys and seven girls served in the alternative instructional treatments for each study. To prevent temporal sequence effects from influencing the results, experimental (and control) variations were studied concurrently within the same time period, as determined by random assignment.

The subject was taken to a room at his school by the adult male experimenter and there was introduced to the adult female model; it should be noted that whereas most subjects were of Mexican-American extraction, both adults were, in appearance, obviously Anglo-Americans. In base line, the experimenter instructed the subject as follows: "I'm going to show you a series of cards. Ask something about each card." Then, "Here is the [next] card, ask something about it," etc.

In each experiment, before the model's performance, the *explicit* instructions treatment was directed as follows: "Now this lady is going to make up a question about each picture. You watch and listen carefully *and try to learn her questions just as well as you can,* and you will have another turn later." The *implicit* instructions omitted the italicized words, but were otherwise identical. After the model's performance, the *explicit* treatment was instructed as follows: "Now you can have another turn to make up questions about each picture. *Try as hard as you can to make your questions like the lady's questions."* The *implicit* instructions omitted the italicized sentence, but were otherwise identical. The model recorded the subject's question responses and hence was present during the entire procedure. Subsequent to readministration of the initial stimuli, the new set of generalization pictures was introduced, without modeling, and *all* subjects received the same instructions as follows: "Here are some new cards. Ask a question about each one."

Each experiment involved a 2 × 3 factorial design, with the implicit and explicit treatments being compared across baseline, imitation, and generalization phases as trials. Given a significant* overall trials effect, Tukey's HSD tests (Kirk, 1968) were used to evaluate the changes from baseline to imitation, from baseline to generalization, and between imitation and generalization phases.

RESULTS

Before discussing the major experimental findings, it is necessary to consider the performance of the no-model control subjects. Initially, two control treatments were studied. In one, the procedures were identical to the implicit instructions treatment, with the omission of demonstration by the model (who was present to record control subjects' responses). In the attempt to deter-

---

* All tests of significance reported in this study were based on *two-*tailed probability estimates.

mine the stability of question categories in response to verbal instructions without modeling, a second no-model control group was instructed, after base line and before readministration of the first set of pictures, as follows: "This time pretend that you are a grown-up when you ask the questions." This attempt to modify control subjects' questions by change-of-role instructions proved to have a rather small effect. By separate analyses of variance for each question category, the two control treatments failed to differ significantly in overall mean frequency of response (largest between-groups $F = 2.75$, $df = 1/26$, $p > .10$). However, some pattern-of-change effects differed in the causal relations and the value judgments question classes, as revealed by significant Groups $\times$ Trials interactions (smaller $F = 3.32$, $df = 2/52$, $p < .05$). When the means for the alternative control treatments were compared, separately within each question class, for baseline, imitation, and generalization phases, using Tukey HSD tests, only the imitation phase means for the value judgments category proved to differ significantly ("implicit" $M = .14$; "instructed" $M = 2.00$, $p < .05$).

It thus appeared that instructions to "pretend that you are a grown-up" had some influence toward increasing the frequency of value judgments questions. Accordingly, as the most conservative option, the two control treatments were combined to form

TABLE 9.1: *Summary of Analyses of Variance across Phases between Implicit and Explicit Groups, and for Groups $\times$ Trials Interaction, within Each Question Class*

Question group	Effects analyzed (F values)		
	Across phases (df = 2/52)	Between groups (df = 1/26)	Groups $\times$ Trials (df = 2/52)
Nominal physical model	24.08**	11.07*	2.43
Functional uses model	35.84**	<1	2.48
Causal relations model	46.75**	<1	<1
Value judgments model	47.07**	<1	<1

    * $p < .01$.
    ** $p < .001$.

the control group for evaluation of "spontaneous" interphase changes. The means by phase for uninstructed, instructed, and pooled control groups are presented elsewhere; all subsequent mention of control results refers to the combined group.

In three question categories, those involving nominal physical, functional uses, and causal relations questions, the pooled control group showed no evidence of change from base line across phases (largest $F = .71$, $df = 2/52$, ns); consequently, there seemed no need to compare experimental subjects' changes from baseline with control group changes in these three variations. However, in the value judgments question class, the control group displayed a numerically small, but statistically significant, increase from baseline across phases ($F = 5.33$, $df = 2/52$, $p < .01$). Therefore, in that study, experimental subjects' changes were evaluated both relative to their own baseline frequencies, and to the controls' changes, in order to demonstrate that modeling had increased the frequency of value judgments questions over and above the increase found among the controls.

Comparisons within Question Classes

For all question category groups, the pattern of results was essentially the same: exposure to the model markedly increased the children's production across phases of each response class modeled; Tukey HSD tests further revealed that changes between baseline and imitation, and between baseline and generalization phases, were separately significant *(largest $p < .01$)*; in no question class did implicit versus explicit instructions interact with change across phases; and the implicit-explicit variation only created a significant between-groups effect (in favor of the explicit instructions) for the nominal physical category. The analyses of variance supporting the foregoing results are summarized in Table 9.1.

Tukey tests further revealed that only the children who observed value judgments questions significantly reduced appropriate response from the imitation to the generalization phase ($p <$

.05). When the value judgments sample (combining implicit and explicit variations which had failed to differ) was compared with the control group, a highly significant between-groups main effect ($F = 23.59$, $df = 1/54$, $p < .001$) in favor of the experimental subjects was found, as well as a significant Groups $\times$ Phases interaction term ($F = 33.17$, $df = 2/108$, $p < .001$). Further analysis of this interaction disclosed that experimental and control subjects did not differ in baseline response, that experimentals' production of value judgments questions surpassed the control group in both imitation and generalization phases (larger $p < .001$), and that although the controls' changes from baseline to imitation and from baseline to generalization were *not* separately significant, the corresponding increases between baseline and each other phase were separately significant for the experimental group (larger $p < .01$). For each question category, the main pattern of results giving the means by phase for combined experimental subjects is presented in Figure 9.1, and the implicit and explicit group means are separately presented elsewhere.

Comparisons between Treatments

In order to further explicate the effects of observing a model display one question class (for example, nominal physical) upon production of the other question categories (for example, value judgments), the four experimental and the control groups (combining implicit and explicit variations) were scored for all question classes studied. For each question class, overall analyses of variance were first performed on the five groups thus composed for the changes from baseline to imitation, and from baseline to generalization phases. Next, the interphase changes in the question formulations of each group were compared with those of each other group by a series of *t* tests; in evaluating these *t*s for descriptive purposes, the .01 level was adopted for significance.

Generally, these analyses revealed that only the group exposed to a relevant model increased its production of the given question category; both from base line to imitation, and to generali-

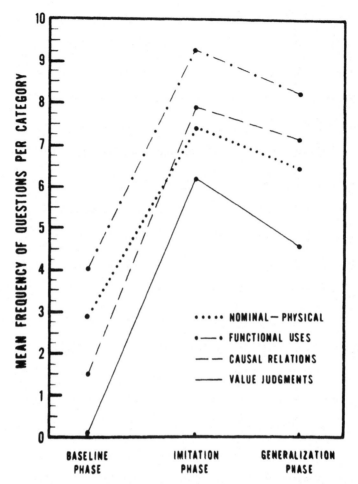

FIGURE 9.1.   Phase means for question categories (combining implicit and explicit instructional treatments), presented for within-variation groups

zation, for every question class the overall analyses of these changes proved highly significant (smallest $F = 14.31$, $df = 4/135$, $p < .001$). Furthermore, the group exposed to modeling of the relevant question category in every comparison significantly surpassed each other group's production of the given question class in all interphase changes (smallest $t = 4.19$, $df = 54$, $p < .001$).

With a constant number of trials, it would be expected that a group's effective adoption of the question class it observed would necessarily reduce its production of the alternative question classes studied. Such a pattern was evident throughout, and as a consequence, the control group (which, for all question categories, showed little change across phases) exceeded the nonrelevant modeling groups in numbers of instances. For example, on functional uses questions, the causal relations and value judgments experimental groups declined from baseline to imitation, and from baseline to generalization, to levels significantly below those of the controls (smallest $t = 2.67$, $p < .01$), whereas the relevant, functional uses modeling group far surpassed the controls in both interphase comparisons (smaller $t = 4.64$, $p < .001$).

In *no* case did observing the model produce given questions covary positively with a different, nonmodeled question class to create significant divergence between irrelevant modeling groups; of 24 such comparisons (across both interphase changes), none approached the 0.1 level, and the largest t obtained barely reached the value necessary for the orthodox $\alpha = .05$ level ($t = 2.17$, $p > .01$).

It should be mentioned that the several groups in general displayed quite comparable baseline means for all question classes. In no instance did any two groups differ significantly, nor did any experimental group tend to surpass any other group in baseline production of the question class it subsequently observed; the largest of such differences involved the value judgments modeling group, whose baseline production of nominal physical questions tended to exceed that of both the relevant, nominal physical modeling group ($t = 2.37$) and of the control group ($t = 2.42$). In essence, then, observing the model produce a particular question class did not appear to enhance by transfer the production of any other of the question classes studied.

Mimicry (Exact Imitation)

For theoretical reasons discussed below, it is important to consider the amount of exact copying, or mimicry, of the model's questions during the imitation phase. For the present analyses, the frequency of exact imitation has been combined *across* experimental variations; the significance tests reported involved comparison of equal numbers of implicit and explicit treatment subjects within each experimental variation, and consequently, differences in the criteria of imitation across the four experiments are equated between the combined implicit and explicit groups. The mean frequency of exact imitation equaled 1.41 for all experimental subjects combined, that is, 11.75% of responses to the 12 stimuli presented. Fully 70.5% of 112 experimental subjects never produced a single copying response; thus, only 29.5% of the children accounted for all mimicry observed. Furthermore, of 158 such copying responses (from a total of 1,344 responses), only 41 (25.9%) were made by children in the implicit instruction treatments. The remaining 74.1% of mimicry responses were produced by the explicit treatments, whose subjects had been instructed to "Try as hard as you can to make your questions like the lady's questions." When mean mimicry for the implicit treatment group ($M = .73$) was compared with that for the explicit group ($M = 2.99$), the results strongly confirmed that the explicit instructions, rather than sheer observation of the model, had played a dominant role in eliciting mimicry ($F = 21.34$, $df = 1/110$, $p < .0001$). The same conclusion resulted when the *proportion* of implicit subjects (.196) who had displayed mimicry was compared with that of explicit subjects (.393) who had mimicked ($CR = 2.29$, $p = 0.2$). Consequently, it seems implausible that the major findings resulted from slavish copying of the model's words; instead, it appeared clear that the children were able to discriminate, and generalize, the criteria governing the model's question classes.

DISCUSSION

The results revealed clearly that children were able to categorize stimuli in accord with the four alternative criteria displayed by the model, and that these bases for information seeking were generalized to new stimuli. The low frequency of exact mimicry of the model's questions, especially by the implicit instructions groups, suggested that children were abstracting the categorical properties of the question classes, and were not merely copying the model's utterances. In this regard, it is interesting that Rosenthal and Whitebook (1970) also found that strong directions to emulate the model increased children's copying of word content, relative to a nondirective procedure, but the divergent instructional groups did not differ in their adoption of the more abstract (tense of verb and kernel sentence pattern) aspects of the model's paradigm. Furthermore, only in one of the four present studies (that involving nominal physical questions) did explicit directions to emulate the model surpass implicit instructional procedures. The data demonstrated that induction (from diverse instances) of abstract criteria governing information seeking represents another example of complex, rule-governed behavior readily subject to vicarious modification. Although the question classes studied differed markedly in their baseline frequencies, significant imitative changes were obtained in each experiment. It appeared noteworthy that these results were generated by a sample of youngsters economically disadvantaged and from homes in which Spanish was, predominantly, the first language learned.

Psycholinguists have tended to confine the concept of imitation to literal mimicry of the model's responses (e.g., Chomsky, 1964; Slobin, 1968). This usage of "imitation" constricts the relevance of social learning contributions to the study of rule-governed behavior (Rosenthal & Whitebook, 1970). In the domain of abstraction and categorization skills, Piaget and his students have exercised a dominant influence. It is difficult to isolate a definitive statement of Piaget's view of imitation. However, the impression is created that he, too, considers imitative learning to involve sheer "reproduction," "mimicking," or an exact "copy" of the model's behavior (e.g., Piaget, 1951, pp. 50–51; 1952, p. 375), and hence to be incapable of transmitting the cognitive organizations which he terms "schemata." Although confirming by replication Bandura and McDonald's (1963) results, current workers in the Piaget tradition (Cowan et al., 1969) have also questioned whether a social-learning position can encompass complexly organized behavior.

Bandura (1969b) has noted these apparent misunderstandings of the conceptual status of imitation within *contemporary* social learning theory, and has elsewhere (1969a, 1969c) discussed in detail the technical information-processing considerations pertaining to a social-learning position. In no sense does this viewpoint confine the study of imitative behavior to narrowly molecular instances in which an observer mimics, or slavishly copies, the exact topography of a model's responses. It is to be hoped that the present studies, and other social-learning research on rule-governed behavior, will help to dispel such an overly limited view of imitative processes.

Skinner (1953) has discussed thought as a refinement of discrimination and generalization responses. Although the present research did not bear on the *de nouveau* development of cognitive structures, the results indicated that social learning procedures were effective in leading children to discriminate the abstract categorizations displayed by the model, and to generalize these classifications to a new set of stimuli. It may be conjectured that whatever factors promote a child's disposition to organize events (e.g., functionally, causally, or valuationally) will exert influence upon enduring habits of organization which he will exhibit. Among such factors, it appears plausible that the typical organizational sets of the persons important in his environment, such as parents and peers, will qualify his organizing behavior in directions not necessarily congruent with hypothetical maturational sequences of cognitive development (e.g., Piaget, 1959, pp. 218–219). In this connection, the present experiments suggest that at least to some degree, the organization of abstraction skills is amenable to change through observational learning.

REFERENCES

BALDWIN, A. L. 1968. *Theories of child development.* New York: Wiley.
BANDURA, A. 1969a. *Principles of behavior modification.* New York: Holt, Rinehart & Winston.

BANDURA, A. 1969b. Social learning of moral judgments. *Journal of Personality and Social Psychology*, 11, 275–279.

BANDURA, A. 1969c. Social-learning theory of identificatory processes. In D. A. Goslin (Ed.), *Handbook of socialization theory and research.* Chicago: Rand McNally.

BANDURA, A., & HARRIS, M. B. 1966. Modification of syntactic style. *Journal of Experimental Child Psychology*, 4, 341–352.

BANDURA, A., & MCDONALD, F. J. 1963. Influence of social reinforcement and the behavior of models in shaping childrens' moral judgments. *Journal of Abnormal and Social Psychology*, 67, 274–281.

CARROLL, W. R., ROSENTHAL, T. L., & BRYSH, C. 1969. Socially induced imitation of grammatical structures. Paper presented at the meeting of the Society for Research in Child Development, Santa Monica, March 1969.

CHOMSKY, N. 1964. Formal discussion. In U. Bellugi & R. W. Brown (Eds.), The acquisition of language. *Monographs of the Society for Research in Child Development*, 29 (1, No. 92), 35–39.

COWAN, P. A., LANGER, J., HEAVENRICH, J., & NATHANSON, M. 1969. Social learning and Piaget's cognitive theory of moral development. *Journal of Personality and Social Psychology*, 11, 261–274.

KIRK, R. E. 1968. *Experimental design: Procedures for the behavioral sciences.* Belmont, Calif.: Brooks/Cole.

ODOM, R. D., LIEBERT, R. M., & HILL, J. H. 1968. The effects of modeling cues, reward, and attentional set on the production of grammatical and ungrammatical syntactic constructions. *Journal of Experimental Child Psychology.* 6, 131–140.

PIAGET, J. 1951. *Play, dreams, and imitation in childhood.* New York: Norton.

PIAGET, J. 1952. *The origins of intelligence in children.* New York: International Universities Press.

PIAGET, J. 1959. *The language and thought of the child.* (3rd ed.) London: Routledge & Kegan-Paul.

ROSENTHAL, T. L., & WHITEBOOK, J. S. 1970. Incentives versus instructions in transmitting grammatical parameters with experimenter as model. *Behaviour Research and Therapy*, 8, 189–196.

SKINNER, B. F. 1953. *Science and human behavior.* New York: Macmillan.

SLOBIN, D. I. 1968. Imitation and grammatical development in children. In N. S. Endler, L. R. Boulter, & H. Osser (Eds.), *Contemporary issues in developmental psychology.* New York: Holt, Rinehart & Winston.

Name Index

203

Subject Index

Affective feedback theory, 12–16, 113

Aggression: learning-performance distinction in, 114; and masculine-role identification, 125; positive reinforcement of, 15, 114–126; punishment of, 15; role of modeling influences in, 114–126; sex differences in, 119, 121, 124–125; vicarious reinforcement of, 6, 114–126

Associative theory: of imitation, 7–8, 25; limitations of, 8

Attention, as influenced by: affective valence of modeling stimuli, 17, 46; arousal level, 17; association preferences of modeling stimuli, 17; complexity of modeling stimuli, 17, 123; distinctiveness of modeling stimuli, 17, 46; functional value of modeling stimuli, 17, 45, 48; past reinforcement, 17, 22–23, 47–48; perceptual set, 17; performance feedback, 40; sensory capacities, 17: in observational learning, 16–17

Classical conditioning theory: affective conditioning in, 12–16; and empathetic learning, 12–13;

of imitation, 12–13, 38, 63–68, 73–87, 113; limitations of, 13–16; proprioceptive feedback in, 14–15

Differentiation of modeling phenomena: and identification, 3–5; in terms of: inhibitory and disinhibitory effects, 6, 30, 151–164; observational learning, 6, 16–26, 30; social facilitation, 6–7, 11–12, 30

Discrimination: of abstract properties, 21, 34, 199–201; in higher order modeling, 33–37; in language learning, 35–36, 182; in matching-to-sample, 11; in observational learning, 11, 17, 34; of response elements, 34; through verbal labeling, 41; through vicarious reinforcement, 36

Disinhibitory effects: on aggression, 6, 125; defined, 6; and model characteristics, 152; and response consequences to the model, 48–50; and transgressive behavior, 6, 151–164; and vicarious extinction, 6, 48

Emotional arousal: and attention, 17; and influence of models, 44,

Lightning Source UK Ltd.
Milton Keynes UK
UKOW01f0628160218
317983UK00001B/20/P